LITURGY IS MISSION

LITURGY IS MISSION

Edited by
FRANK STEPHEN CELLIER

NEW YORK   1964

ACKNOWLEDGMENTS

Grateful acknowledgment is made to the following authors and publishers for permission to use copyrighted material from the titles listed:

Harcourt, Brace & World, Inc.—T. S. Eliot, *Four Quartets*
New Directions—Dylan Thomas, *Collected Poems of Dylan Thomas*

PUBLISHED IN ASSOCIATION WITH
THE ASSOCIATED PARISHES FOR LITURGY AND MISSION

*To the men and women of
the Christian Diaspora
who in liturgical confrontation
find the meeting ground which is
Christ, their Lord and their God.*

CONTENTS

THE CONTRIBUTORS

FRANK STEPHEN CELLIER is Lecturer in Liturgics at Seabury-Western Theological Seminary; and Executive Producer, Informational Programs, Sears, Roebuck and Co. He is a member of the Associated Parishes for Liturgy and Mission, and is Secretary to The Standing Liturgical Commission.

THE REV. W. MOELWYN MERCHANT, sometime Senior Lecturer in English at Cardiff, Wales, now heads the Department of English at Exeter University in England. As a well-known Shakespearean scholar he has lectured in many American universities. He is prominent in the field of religious drama and is well acquainted with some leading writers, musicians, and artists of our day.

THE REV. C. KILMER MYERS is Director of the Urban Training Center, Chicago. He has been a pioneer in the inner-city ministry at Grace Church, Van Vorst, Jersey City, and as Vicar of the Chapel of the Intercession, Trinity Parish, New York City, one of the largest racially integrated churches in the country. He is the author of *Light the Dark Streets*, which deals with his ministry to New York street gangs. A graduate of Rutgers University and Berkeley Divinity School, he taught at the General Theological Seminary, New York.

THE REV. JOSEPH THOMAS NOLAN is pastor of St. Patrick's Roman Catholic parish at Galena, Kansas, and St. Joseph's

parish at Baxter Springs, Kansas. He is well known as an
author and speaker in the liturgical movement of the Roman Catholic Church, and has served as a member of the
Board of Directors of the National Liturgical Conference.
Father Nolan received an A.B. from Boston College in 1942,
and an M.A. from Boston College in 1949. In the intervening years he served as an officer in the U.S. Navy and as a
Special Agent in the Federal Bureau of Investigation. He
entered Immaculate Conception Seminary at Conception,
Missouri, in 1949 and was ordained to the priesthood in
1953. He writes frequently on pastoral and liturgical subjects and has published many aids to parish liturgical life.

THE RT. REV. JAMES A. PIKE, Bishop of the Protestant Episcopal Diocese of California, is a graduate of the University
of Southern California, Yale Law School, and Union Theological Seminary. Admitted to the practice of law in California and before the United States Supreme Court, he
taught at George Washington University Law School and
was also Adjunct Professor of Religion and Law at Colum-
bia University. He has served as seminary tutor, college
chaplain, and Dean of the Cathedral of St. John the Divine,
New York. Long interested in the relation of worship to
daily life and in Christian social relations, Bishop Pike is
a popular preacher, lecturer, and television interviewer.
Among his books are *Doing the Truth, Beyond Anxiety,*
and *If You Marry Outside Your Faith;* he is also co-author
of *The Faith of the Church* and editor of *Modern Canterbury Pilgrims.* Bishop Pike has served as a member of the
Department of Religious Liberty of the National Council
of Churches, the California Advisory Committee to the
U.S. Commission on Civil Rights, and the U.S. Food for

Peace Council, and he was recently decorated by the State of Israel.

THE REV. WILLIAM G. POLLARD is Executive Director of the Oak Ridge Institute of Nuclear Studies and Priest-in-Charge of St. Alban's Chapel, Clinton, Tennessee. He was Professor of Physics at the University of Tennessee from 1936 to 1947, except for two years of work on the Manhattan Project. He has held his present position since 1947, and he was ordained priest in 1954. He is the co-author of *The Hebrew Iliad* and author of *Chance and Providence* and *Physicist and Christian*.

THE REV. MASSEY H. SHEPHERD, JR., Professor of Liturgics at The Church Divinity School of the Pacific, Berkeley, California, is one of the best known liturgical scholars of the Anglican Communion. He received his higher education at the University of South Carolina, the University of Chicago, and the Berkeley Divinity School. He is a member of The Standing Liturgical Commission of the Episcopal Church, The American Society of Church History, and The Associated Parishes for Liturgy and Mission. His articles and books include: *The Worship of the Church, At All Times and in All Places, The Paschal Liturgy and the Apocalypse, The Reform of Liturgical Worship, The Living Liturgy,* and *The Oxford American Prayer Book Commentary*.

LITURGY IS MISSION

INTRODUCTION

by

the Editor

The contemporary Reformation in the Church—Roman, Anglican, Protestant, and Orthodox—is much less spectacular but in many ways as significant as the Reformation of the sixteenth century. Perhaps even more so.

THE LITURGICAL MOVEMENT

This reformation is generally referred to as the Liturgical Movement, and a good name it is, too. For today's Church has been discovering slowly, but surely, that liturgy is the key to its getting back in tune with the times by proclaiming the immutable truth of the Gospel in words which are as comfortable to the twentieth century as earlier words were to the first.

We had, of course, been gradually getting out of tune with our times. We found that we no longer were in phase with the world to the degree that we had been in—say—the seventeenth century. Most of us would date the Church's desegregation from society (particularly intellectual society) to the so-called Age of Enlightenment—

what the Germans in their inimitable fashion call the
Aufklärung (clearing up). Actually, the word should be
Ausklärung (clearing out)!

However that may be, the Church has been on the de-
fensive ever since; but as it tried in the Wesley era, so in
our own twentieth century the Church is trying to seek out
the world and speak a word of compelling relevance to its
men and women.

The stirring of God's people's deep concern for the kerygmatic mission of the Church, irrespective of Confession, can
properly be called a Movement—"spontaneous and unre-
hearsed," as they say on radio and television.

It can perhaps be summarized in one sentence: as the
Church once conquered the known world through its liturgy, so it can do again today—if only it will make the
saving gospel of life and death and victory with Christ
and in Christ *nuclear* to the lives of the men and women
who, consciously or otherwise, yearn to respond to God's
grace by doing what the Greeks called their *leitourgia*, their
service.

The concern of the Liturgical Movement is summed up
by the titles of such books as A. G. Hebert's prognostic
Liturgy and Society, Louis Bouyer's *Liturgical Piety*, Jean
Danielou's *The Bible and the Liturgy*, and Massey Shepherd's *The Liturgical Renewal of the Church*. The title of
the present book reflects that same concern.

What the men of the Liturgical Movement are saying is
that the liturgy must rest four-square on biblical founda-
tions; that it always has been and always will be the supreme channel of God's grace to the individual; and that
the individual reflects the efficacy of his reception of God's

grace by the way in which he confronts the society he lives in.

The Liturgical Movement is profoundly aware that the Christian can witness adequately to his Lord and Saviour only "after that he has received power"—the enabling power which will make it possible for him to carry out the injunction of that same Lord and Saviour. "Go ye therefore, and teach all nations . . ." (Matt. 28:19) "Be witnesses unto me both in Jerusalem, and in all Judaea, and in Samaria, and unto the uttermost part of the earth." (Acts 1:8)

This profound awareness on the part of the Liturgical Movement merely reflects the experience of the Church from that day when the disciples had gone up into the mountain with their risen Lord, and a cloud had come, and when the cloud had disappeared, he had disappeared too.

They had been told to go back to Jerusalem and wait. The record is not clear that they knew exactly what it was they were waiting for, even though their Lord had said to them:

> If I go not away, the Comforter will not come unto you. . . . But when the Comforter is come, whom I will send unto you from the Father, even the Spirit of truth, which proceedeth from the Father, he shall testify of me; and ye also shall bear witness. (John 16:7; 15:26-27)

So, we are told, they "returned to Jerusalem with great joy; and were continually in the temple praising and blessing God" (Luke 24:52-53), in preparation for the Power that was to come upon them and would enable them to bear witness throughout the then known world, frequently unto death.

The Liturgical Movement is grounded on this very principle: the worship of God precedes man's witness in the world. For this reason the literature of the Liturgical Movement dwells with deep and profound emphasis on worship and the nature of worship as such.[1]

The emphasis on *worship first,* and *action second,* is, of course, a reflection of our Lord's Summary of the Law: first, "Love the Lord thy God;" and then (but only then) "Love thy neighbor." It is similarly a reflection of the exordium of the prayer which the Lord Christ himself taught us to pray.[2]

First we say, "Hallowed be thy name." In other words, first we worship. Then, and only then, do we say "Thy kingdom come." It is only after we have raised our hearts and minds to God in complete adoration that we receive the power and (as we say it nowadays) the "know-how" to work for the spread of God's kingdom on earth.

It is natural, therefore, that the Liturgical Movement should be deeply concerned with the nature of man's worship. The records are, of course, perfectly clear that from the earliest times the Church gathered in the fellowship of what the Prayer Book calls "the blessed company of all faithful people" for the purpose of "doing this in remembrance of me." The Lord's Day was pre-eminently the day on which the Church, from the beginning, gathered to celebrate what St. Paul calls "the Lord's Supper" (I Cor. 11:20). In subsequent centuries this great weekly banquet of the Lord came to be known by various names. Some learned to call it the Divine Liturgy; others, the Mass;

[1] See, for example, Evelyn Underhill, *Worship* (New York: Harper & Bros., 1937).

[2] See Bishop Lichtenberger's Paper in Massey H. Shepherd, *The Liturgical Renewal of the Church* (New York: Oxford, 1960), p. 103.

others, the Holy Communion; and yet others, the Holy
Eucharist.

But by whatever name the Church's supreme act of worship is called, the men of the Liturgical Movement are most
seriously convinced that for a member of Christ's Body to
enter adequately into his calling he should seize every opportunity to become joined to the Head of the Body in this
heavenly banquet where time and eternity meet.

The men and women in the worshiping congregation
live *in a world of time.* The Lord Christ, who conquered
death and who sitteth at the right hand of the Father, *"ever
liveth* to make intercession for them" (Heb. 7:25). In the
Eucharist the faithful offer and present themselves, their
souls, their bodies, to be a reasonable, holy, and living sacrifice unto God. They conjoin the sacrifice of all they are
now, all they have, and all they have been (good or bad),
and all they hope to be, with Christ's own eternally valid
oblation of himself, once offered.

The Holy Eucharist is a recalling,* an *anamnesis,* of his
saving ministry on earth, "his blessed passion and precious
death, his mighty resurrection and glorious ascension."
Assimilating ourselves into the life, death, resurrection, and
ascension of our Lord leads us to pray in the Holy Eucharist
that "we may evermore dwell in him, and he in us."

Having what St. Paul calls a "communion in the blood of
Christ . . . and in the body of Christ" (I Cor. 10:16) is the
most profound experience which the Christian can undergo.
For this reason, it is only natural that the men of the Liturgical Movement should be deeply concerned with the words

* I am indebted for this usage to the Most Reverend Leslie W. Brown,
Archbishop of Uganda, who incorporated it into the African Draft
Liturgy (1963).

which are spoken by both celebrant and people in the Divine Liturgy, by the music which is sung, by the physical arrangements of the church, and by the ceremonial which frames the entire action. In the main, this concern has taken the form of delving deeply into the oldest accounts of how the apostolic and sub-apostolic Church performed the Divine Liturgy.

The most ancient source is, of course, the New Testament itself—sparse as the accounts may be. From the three Synoptic Gospels (Matt. 26:26-28; Mark 14:22-24; and Luke 22:19-20) and from St. Paul's First Epistle to the Corinthians (11:23-25), it is clear that when our Lord instituted the Last Supper, he first *gave thanks*. Most modern scholars believe that the form of consecratory blessing which our Lord used over the bread and the wine was in much the same form as it still appears in the Jewish Prayer Book: "Blessed art thou, O Lord our God, King of the universe, who bringest forth bread from the earth . . . [and] createst the fruit of the vine." [3] We know that after having taken the bread and consecrated it by a prayer of thanksgiving, he next broke it and gave it to his disciples saying, "Take eat: This is my body which is broken for you: This do in remembrance of me." And that after having taken the cup and consecrated it by a prayer of thanksgiving, he gave it to them saying, "Drink ye all of it; For this is my blood of the new covenant which is shed for many for the remission of sins: This do ye, as oft as ye drink it, in remembrance of me."

Another ancient source of major significance is the *Apology of Justin Martyr* which was written in the middle of the second century and gives a brief but invaluable account of

[3] *Authorized Daily Prayer Book,* Revised Edition. Dr. Joseph H. Hertz (New York: Block Publishing Company, 1961), p. 409.

a celebration of the Holy Eucharist in a secret place at the time when the Church was enduring the severity of its early persecution.

Perhaps the most valuable ancient source of all is the document known as the *Apostolic Tradition of Hippolytus,* which was written during the first quarter of the third century. Here we find the consecratory thanksgiving much elaborated and leading naturally into our Lord's Words of Administration: "Take, eat: This is my Body. . . . Drink ye: This is my Blood."

The form of Hippolytus' Eucharistic prayer furthermore includes (although some scholars are somewhat doubtful as to the originality of this portion) an Invocation to the Holy Ghost, suggestive of the *Epiclesis* for which the Eastern Liturgies are so notable.

In the course of time, the Church in the West came more and more to regard the Dominical Words, "This is my Body . . . This is my Blood" as the "moment" of consecration; while the Eastern Church came to regard the Invocation to the Holy Ghost (the *Epiclesis*) as the "moment" of consecration. The Liturgical Movement recognizes no "moment" of consecration. It finds that it is the *entire action* of the Eucharist which consecrates. For this reason the men of the Liturgical Movement seek above all to involve all of God's people in the whole of the Church's greatest act of worship. If all of God's people are to unite in their response to God's summons, "Love the Lord thy God with all thy heart and all thy soul and all thy mind, [and] Praise the Lord, O my soul, and all that is within me, praise his holy name" (Matt. 22:37; Ps. 103:1) then, quite obviously, the Divine Liturgy cannot serve its function if it becomes a mere spectacle to which people go as they do to a ballet performance where there is interesting choreography and attractive music, but in which they, as audience, are relegated to the role of mere onlookers.

Penetrating and crucial considerations of this type have been and continue to be the deep and prayerful concern of liturgiologists: whether Roman Catholics like Father Nolan, Anglicans like Dr. Shepherd, Lutherans like Dr. Piepkorn, members of the Orthodox Church like Dr. Schmemann, or men from a dozen other persuasions.

Men like these are concerned with such matters as performing the Liturgy in what Archbishop Cranmer called "a language understanded of the people"; translating the Mass (or at least parts of it) into the vernacular; saying the great Consecration Prayer audibly (since the *disciplina arcani* has even less relevance to today's world than the Stanley Steamer). These men are concerned with reintroducing into the liturgical drama the "altar in the round" (or free-standing at least, as in ancient basilicas), giving all the people of God the sense of having the Mystery take place in their very midst instead of far away at a sarcophagus-altar placed snugly against the east wall, which can be seen from the nave of a great church about as dimly as one can see the second act of *Tristan and Isolde* from the family circle in the Metropolitan Opera House. They stress the value of having an offertory procession in which representatives of the congregation bear to the altar the bread and the wine which are the symbols of the daily endeavor of us all—not because the custom happens to be ancient, but because, if properly understood, such a procession integrates the lives of God's people more closely into the dramatic action of the altar-sacrament where their own imperfect lives are intermingled and united with the perfect life of their Lord and Saviour. These liturgiologists emphasize the significance of having a gospel procession in which the record of the Good News is carried closer to the people of God, the better to symbolize their appropriation of it for themselves.

There are large numbers of people in our own Anglican Church (and I am by no means excluding any one of the four orders: bishops, priests, deacons, and laymen) whose awareness of the Liturgical Movement is so flimsy that they equate a mere ceremony, such as an offertory procession or a gospel procession, with the Liturgical Movement itself. If such ceremonies are introduced into a parish without a careful, *pastoral* exposition of their symbolic significance they become mere forms and are in no sense representative of what the Liturgical Movement is trying to achieve.

In sum, therefore, the Liturgical Movement has its roots very deep in the soil of an *ecclesiology* which conceives of all members of the Church as having been "called of Jesus Christ" in their capacity of *peculia* or especial possessions of God (I Pet. 2:9) to bear witness to him in whatever nook and cranny of the world they may happen to find themselves.

It has its roots very deep in the soil of a *sacramental theology* which sees clearly that God mediates his grace through his creatures—whether animal or vegetable or mineral. It sees what Odo Casel has called "mystery theology" (*Mysterien-theologie*) as one profound explanation of what takes place both objectively and subjectively in the Sacrament of the Holy Eucharist.

Finally, and most importantly, the Liturgical Movement has its roots deep in the soil of *pastoral theology*, with especial emphasis on the homiletical and exegetical function of the minister in his parish. His people, no less than he himself, must know precisely what it is they are doing, what they are engaged in, in the Church's greatest act of worship. The meaning of every action and of every word must be clearly understood and thoroughly assimilated by both celebrant and people before the Eucharist can become the single most important experience in the life of every professing Christian.

THE ASSOCIATED PARISHES

In the American Branch of the Anglican Communion, the Liturgical Movement is spearheaded by an organization known as The Associated Parishes for Liturgy and Mission.

This organization is not to be confused with the Church's Standing Liturgical Commission, which derives its purpose and function from the General Convention of the Church. It is the task of this Commission to assess the mind of the Church in regard to the liturgy as contained in the Book of Common Prayer. From time to time, the Standing Liturgical Commission publishes *Prayer Book Studies,* each of which contains an interpretative essay, reflecting the Commission's understanding of the thinking of all segments of the Church and making proposals for modifications in existing Prayer Book services.

These *Studies* are intended to do what their title suggests: namely, to give the Church an opportunity for further reflection on the liturgy in question, be it the Daily Offices, the Ministration of Holy Baptism, the Order of Confirmation, the Form of Solemnization of Matrimony, the Order for the Visitation of the Sick, the Order for the Burial of the Dead, the Ordinal, or, last but not least, the Holy Eucharist itself.

Unlike the Standing Liturgical Commission, the Associated Parishes for Liturgy and Mission has no official standing in the Church. It is a voluntary association of some thirty priests of the Church and a few laymen. It was formed spontaneously some seventeen years ago by a number of men who committed themselves to what is called today "A Parish Program for Liturgy and Mission"—a program of putting into actual practice the aims of the worldwide, supra-confessional Liturgical Movement. Each member of the Associated Parishes for Liturgy and Mission (or "AP," as it is commonly called) undertakes to introduce the principles of the Liturgical Movement into his particular sphere of activity—be it a parish, a seminary, or the business world.

AP has extended its missionary reach beyond the immediate vocational environment of any single one of its members. It has done so in two notable ways: first, by publishing a number of attractive booklets; and, second, by conducting a series of national liturgical conferences.

The booklets which AP has published during the seventeen years of its existence, or is currently preparing for publication, deal with such subjects as the Holy Eucharist, the Daily Offices, Liturgy and Work, Holy Matrimony, and Christian Initiation. These booklets are interpretative in both word and picture.

To date, AP has conducted three National Liturgical Conferences.

The Madison Liturgical Conference, 1958

The papers read at the Madison Liturgical Conference were edited by the Rev. Dr. Massey Hamilton Shepherd and were published by the Oxford University Press in 1960 under the title, *The Liturgical Renewal of the Church.*

The addresses covered a wide range of subjects. The Rev. Dr. Theodore Otto Wedel, sometime Warden of the College of Preachers, discussed "The Theology of the Liturgical Renewal," drawing particular attention to the Mystery Theology of Dom Odo Casel of the Abbey of Maria Laach. Some of Dom Casel's main contributions have recently been collected by B. Neunheuser and published in an English translation entitled *The Mystery of Christian Worship* (Westminster, Md.: Newman Press, 1962).

Dr. Shepherd gave the Conference an extensive survey of the "History of the Liturgical Renewal." While he devoted most of his time to a discussion of the course which the Liturgical Movement has taken in the Roman Catholic Church, he pointed out that its principal manifestation in the Anglican Communion has been that of Prayer Book revision.

The Rev. Dr. Arthur Carl Piepkorn of the Concordia (Lutheran) Seminary in St. Louis, Missouri, addressed himself to the "Protestant Worship Revival and the Lutheran Liturgical Movement." It should be pointed out that at each of the three National Liturgical Conferences sponsored by AP thus far, at least one of the speakers has been an eminent liturgiologist from a Confession not in communion with the Anglican branch of the Church. This is no accident. Speakers like these are invited so that the in-

terconfessional nature of the dialogue of Liturgical Renewal
will be emphasized.

The Rt. Rev. Arthur Carl Lichtenberger, now Presiding
Bishop of the Protestant Episcopal Church in America, re-
viewed the "Social Implications of the Liturgical Renewal."
Referring to Cardinal Gasquet's story of the priest who said
that the layman in the Church had but two positions: kneel-
ing at Mass, and sitting when the priest was in the pulpit,
Bishop Lichtenberger urged the Conference to realize that
after the Christian had partaken of the Holy Mysteries of
the altar, his function was to become a channel through
which God would, with his own redeeming power and in
his own time, transform the world.

The Rev. Dr. John Oliver Patterson, speaking out of his
long experience as Rector of Grace Church in Madison and
Headmaster of Kent School in Connecticut, gave the Conference an overview of the "Pastoral Implications of the
Liturgical Renewal." He emphasized the need for restoring
the Eucharist to a position of centrality in the Church's
worship and stressed the inescapable duty which rests upon
the priest to make his parishioners thoroughly conversant
with the vast theological significance of the Divine Liturgy
for their own personal lives.

At the Choral Eucharist which climaxed the Conference,
the Rev. Dr. William Hamilton Nes of Seabury-Western
Theological Seminary preached a sermon which he called
"The Word for Ascensiontide": the "waiting time" between
the Day of Ascension and the Day of Pentecost. He looked
with wit, piety, and acumen at the Liturgical Movement
as a stirring of God's Holy Spirit in the hearts of all men
who call themselves Christians, in order that their commit-

ment might be complete both to the Lord Christ and to the
fact that his gospel is for all men in all times and in all
places.

The San Antonio Liturgical Conference, 1959

The addresses given at AP's second National Liturgical
Conference were also edited by Dr. Shepherd and were published by the Oxford University Press in 1960 under the
title, *The Eucharist and Liturgical Renewal.*

The opening address was delivered by the Rt. Rev.
Stephen F. Bayne, Jr., Executive Officer of the Anglican
Communion. He called his address "The Eucharist and the
Church" and pointed to the dual tradition in the history of
the Church: the preoccupation with *time,* and the preoccupation with *timelessness.* Each of these traditions is a noble
heritage from the 2,000 years of our Lord.

These two traditions of the Church should be thought of
as complementary. As the Christian *lives* the eucharistic
Liturgy he will naturally and inevitably sanctify time by
praising and worshiping God in the Daily Offices. And, as
the most natural act of sublime worship, he will join himself into the timelessness of Christ's Sacrifice by communicating at the altar as often as possible.

The Rev. Dr. John Marshall Holt, then of the Episcopal
Theological Seminary of the Southwest, addressed himself
to "The Eucharist and the Bible." The relationship, he
made clear, is intimate and inseparable. Pointing to the
profound role which the Bible has played in the American
ethos, Dr. Holt emphasized that the Logos is the dominant
characteristic of the Eucharist. "When ethos assumes the
dominance over Logos, the most sour and fault-finding
moralism results," he said. Our ethical culture, in the last

analysis, will depend on the completeness with which we receive the Word in the Holy Eucharist and identify ourselves with him.

Dr. Dora Phyllis Chaplin of the General Theological Seminary presented to the Conference an unusually sensitive paper, "The Eucharist and Education." She pleaded for the essential necessity that faces every Christian to relate the sublime experience of the Eucharist to the entirety of God's creation. God channels his grace to his people through persons and things, and above all, to those who unite the sacrifice of their lives—their failures, their triumphs, their hopes, their fears—to Christ's oblation of himself once offered. Everyone who comes to Holy Communion, she pointed out, should be educated to the fact that in Christopher Fry's words:

> The enterprise
> Is exploration into God.

The problem of Christian education is, in sum, the problem of teaching all communicants to have a reverence for all of life; to cultivate a foundation for right belief; to grasp thoroughly the shape of the Eucharistic Liturgy; to be realistic about the problem of meaninglessness in modern times; and, finally, to understand the sacramental principle far better than it is understood by the vast majority of Christians.

Dr. Wilford Oakland Cross, then of the University of the South and now of Nashota House, discussed "The Economic and Social Implications of the Eucharist." He pointed out that the ethical principles of daily Christian living are immanent in the Eucharist; but must not be searched for, textually. The Eucharist is a "marvellous poem of praise

and thanksgiving." However, the very doing of the Divine
Liturgy inevitably becomes the profound resolve to fulfill
God's will from moment to moment for the simple and ob-
vious reason that it is a bounden duty and service. As
Guardini puts it, he said, through the Eucharist "the indi-
vidual is as one of the people." [4]

When the Body of Christ offers thanksgiving for creation
and redemption to the Father, the social doctrine which is
implied throughout is that all men are a brotherhood without race, class, or status, and hence is affirmed the sacredness
of the human personality. The sacrifice of his own life and
work which man makes in the Eucharist is symbolized in
the elements of bread and wine. They are tokens not only
of man's labor but also of his sin; not only of what he has
done but also what he has left undone. At the altar the
bread is made holy in brotherhood and peace. The social
implications of the Eucharist are that our daily bread is
similarly to be hallowed by the way we acquit ourselves in
the market place.

Dr. Frank Stephen Cellier, editor of the present book,
urged the Conference to be aware of the challenge which
the Liturgical Movement presents to the Church for the
effective "Ministry of the Laity." He stressed the fact that
the laity are in a unique position to proclaim the kerygma
in word and deed to the world in which they live and work;
but he emphasized that, particularly in our pelagian Anglo-
Saxon culture, they need to be adequately equipped for the
task of witness. The layman must be brought to realize beyond any doubt that he has no power of himself to help
himself; that he cannot do anything that is good without

[4] Romano Guardini, *The Church and the Catholic* (New York:
Sheed and Ward, 1935), p. 28.

God; that for this reason he must constantly beseech God to "prevent" and follow him with his grace, mercifully granting that his Holy Spirit may in all things direct and rule his heart and mind. Once the layman becomes profoundly convinced of this, his witness follows inevitably.

The Very Rev. Dr. Alexander Schmemann of St. Vladimir's Orthodox Seminary in New York delivered what was perhaps the most arresting address of the entire Conference. Reflecting the ancient and consistent tradition of the great Eastern Churches, he transported the Conference into the eschatological dimension of the Eucharist, where men and women together with angels and archangels join on the "eighth day"—a day which is out of time and in eternity— in a paean of worship to the God who is holy, who is holy and strong, who is holy and immortal. Christ not only descends to be present on the earthly altar but the whole Body ascends with him to be present at the heavenly altar.

The San Antonio Conference concluded with a choral Eucharist at which the Rt. Rev. John P. Craine, Bishop of Indianapolis, preached a sermon on "The Eucharistic Life." Bishop Craine emphasized the fact that one is not a Christian of his own choosing. Rather, he is chosen by God. As Jesus said to his Disciples, "Ye have not chosen me, but I have chosen you, and ordained you." (John 15:16)

Bishop Craine went on to point out that, once chosen, man has no option but obedience, which demands an immense faithfulness on his part. Here the Church and its discipline are an immense source of sustenance. This sustenance is given particularly through the sacramental grace which the Christian receives in the Eucharist. Finally, the sheer participation in the Holy Communion is not the end of anything but rather the beginning of everything. One is to go forth from the Eucharist and, with the power that God has vouchsafed him, relate all men to God, and extend the life of Christ the Lord into all of the world.

The Wichita Liturgical Conference, 1962

The third and most recent National Liturgical Conference sponsored by AP was held in Wichita, Kansas. The host parish in this case was St. James' Church in Wichita. These national liturgical conferences have to date been held under the sponsorship of AP with the unstinting cooperation of a host parish whose rector is a member of AP. In this case the rector was the Reverend Frederick W. Putnam, president of AP, who subsequently has been consecrated Bishop Suffragan of Oklahoma. The attendance at the Conference exceeded 950 persons; they had come from 46 states.

The Conference was addressed by men of singular distinction, all of them with the invigorating wind of the Liturgical Movement blowing full in their faces. The chapters of this book are based on the contributions of these men, who made the Wichita Conference such an outstanding milestone in the liturgical thinking of the Church.

Chapter I, "Liturgy and Mission," is based on the keynote address, which was delivered by Dr. Massey Shepherd, and from the thesis of which the title of the present book is taken.

Chapter II, "The Liturgical Movement in the Roman Catholic Church," is taken from the paper delivered to the Conference by Father Joseph Nolan. His penetrating and irenical address was subsequently described by Dr. Merchant as "graceful, gay, and profound." All the Conference rejoiced in the fact that he delivered his address in the presence of his bishop, the Most Rev. Mark W. Carroll of Wichita.

Chapter III, "The Church's Mission to the Artist," is based on the paper delivered to the Conference by Dr. Moelwyn Merchant, whose Gaelic mind is poetry and fire and charity—all at the same time.

Chapter IV is based on the paper, "The Church's Mission to a Scientific Culture," delivered to the Conference by Dr. William Pollard, priest-scientist, to whose mind the Nicene Creed is as the nucleus to the atom.

Chapter V, "The Liturgy and Work," is taken from the classically *multum in parvo* sermon delivered by Bishop Pike of California at the Choral Eucharist with which the final day of the Conference opened triumphantly.

Chapter VI is based on "The Church's Mission to Our Urban Society," the address to the Conference by Dr. Kilmer Myers, whose Christian urbanism forges saving links between the despair of the street and the altar of God.

The Conference closed on a note of high optimism that the Church's concern with matters liturgical was, indeed, an earnest of its desire to reassume the ancient kerygmatic obligation which it owes more than ever to the world of the later twentieth century.

CHAPTER I

LITURGY AND MISSION

by

Massey H. Shepherd, Jr.

To speak of liturgy and mission within the compass of a single chapter is to attempt in a short space a synopsis of Christianity twice. For liturgy and mission are but two names for the same reality. Both terms describe the Church's manifestation in and to the world in the here and now: that single and final revelation of God in Christ for man's salvation. Both liturgy and mision make evident that givenness of grace for the restoration of humanity in communion with God, which is occasion for our repentance, faith, charity, and obedience.

THE PRESENT FORM OF GOD'S ACTION
IN CHRIST

This past summer a student of mine presented in his term paper assignment, which was a definition of the liturgy, an unusually apt and succinct statement: namely, that "the liturgy is the present form of God's action in Christ." The same definition could be used without any change of word-

ing for the Church's missionary witness. This is exactly
what St. Paul understood the gospel to be, including his
own vocation to its proclamation, when he described it as:

> the preaching [kerygma] of Jesus Christ, according to
> the revelation of the mystery which was kept secret for
> long ages but is now disclosed and through the pro-
> phetic writings is made known to all nations, according
> to the command of the eternal God, to bring about
> obedience to the faith. (Romans 16:25-26)

Liturgy and mission are the making present here and now
of the once-for-all, accomplished self-offering and triumph
of God in his only beloved and perfectly obedient Son.
They are at the same time our incorporation and participation in his merits and in his glory.

Liturgy and mission "are the present form of God's action
in Christ." This perspective must be stressed again and
again. We are always so prone to fall into the fallacy of
thinking of liturgy and mission as something which *we* do.
Because both liturgy and mission are the sphere of our
response and obedience to God's summons, we are apt to
stress the importance of our response more than the grace
of our summons. The language of psalmody comes readily
to our lips: "bring presents, and come into his courts"—
this is our action in worship; "tell it out among the heathen
that the Lord is King"—this is our action in witness. But
the very same psalm from which these responses are taken
(Psalm 96) contains the proper context: "for the Lord is
great, and cannot worthily be praised . . . . it is he who
hath made the round world . . . . and he shall judge the
peoples righteously."

Never is God or Christ or the Holy Spirit the passive
object of our service or of anything that we do, but rather

the active Subject who serves us, and in us serves mankind. The great exordium of the Collect for the Twelfth Sunday after Trinity has the root of the matter: "Almighty and everlasting God, who art always more ready to hear than we to pray, and art wont to give more than either we desire or deserve." Whenever we speak of worship or of witness as a "service"—and what better word so singly and perfectly describes them both?—we must know that it is not our service but *his* service. This is why both liturgy and mission are for us such hard and arduous work. It is because the terms of this service are not of our making but of God's. We do not appease him; he reconciles us. We do not change God; he transforms us. God cannot be put upon and used. This fact distinguishes true Christian service from non-Christian or sub-Christian service. And this fact preserves the Christian from all anxiety and frustration, for these sins arise from the promptings and attempts to manipulate God. He does not ask us to succeed, but to be faithful.

Recently two manuscripts on liturgical themes have crossed my desk in preparation for publication. The authors of both of them are men of sincerity and devotion, deeply concerned for the dignity and meaning of true worship. But in each case, they have fallen unwittingly, as all of us constantly fall, into the same easy fallacy. In one of these booklets, an instruction on worship for children, there occurred the naked sentence: "Worship is something that we do for God." In the other, a guide for wedding ceremonies, the couple are carefully reminded that at their marriage in the Church, God is there as a "guest." But if God is a guest in his own house, who is the host?

In our Lord's parables of the Kingdom in which he describes the Kingdom as a great feast—as the Messianic,

Eucharistic banquet—he did not say that a committee
planned the feast and invited the King as an honored
guest, and placed him at the head table on the right hand
of the committee chairman. On the contrary, the King himself made all the arrangements, issued all the invitations,
and decided himself what would be the seating accommo-
dations. The guests had nothing to do but accept and be
graciously served—and served indeed, way and beyond their
deserving or their expectations.

LITURGY IS MISSION

The scandal of every Eucharist is the scandal of the Last
Supper. Jesus serves us first. And we cannot save him or
protect him from this menial task. So the Church, like its
spokesman Peter, recoils in amazement: "Lord, dost thou
wash my feet?"

> So after he had washed their feet, and had taken his
> garments, and was set down again, he said unto them,
> Know ye what I have done to you? Ye call me Master
> and Lord: and ye say well; for so I am. If I then, your
> Lord and Master, have washed your feet; ye also ought
> to wash one another's feet. For I have given you an
> example, that ye should do as I have done to you.
> Verily, verily, I say unto you, The servant is not greater
> than his lord; neither he that is sent greater than he
> that sent him. If ye know these things, happy are ye
> if ye do them. (John 13:12-17)

That is liturgy and mission. How can they be separated?
There is, to be sure, a difference of form, just as the
blessing and giving of bread and wine is different in form
from the washing and wiping of feet. In the liturgy, the
Church's immediate environment is heaven and its attention is focused in the heavenly realm. In the liturgy, we are

with Christ the ascended Lord, in the midst of the whole
company of angels and archangels and saints. We are en-
gulfed in adoration and praise, surrounded by doxology
and *Sanctus*. There we feast upon the marriage Supper of
the Lamb. There we voice with all creation the ineffable
Benedicite, whose "sound goes out into all lands and its
words unto the ends of the world." (Romans 10:18) In its
mission, the Church's attention is more immediately earth-
ward—reaching out to the world of men, to the least of
Christ's brethren for whom he died and shed his blood.
In the mission the Church loses its life as he lost his. In
the mission the Church gathers up, communicates, distrib-
utes, at the very least, the precious crumbs that have fallen
from the Master's table.

Yet in neither the liturgy nor the mission, it must be
noted, is the Church centered upon itself, inwardly cul-
tivating its own existence and its own maintenance. The
Church is never an end in itself. In the seer's vision of ultimate fulfillment in the City of God—that city coming down
from heaven—there is no Church. Nor is there any word or
sacrament, only the Lamb mediating between God and his
people. The Church and its ministries of word and sacrament are means, means which derive their meaning and
purpose only in that to which they witness—the transcendent Kingdom of God where Christ is Lord of all.

Neither the liturgy nor the mission of the Church are of
its own ecclesiastical creation. The liturgy is given by the
Lord's institution, with the express purpose that it be done
to *remember* him. The mission is given by the Lord's commission, with the express purpose that it be done to *proclaim* him. It is necessary to affirm these truths over and
over again. The Church possesses the mysteries of word and

sacrament only as a steward; their ownership belongs only
and solely to Christ. The Church will be judged not by the
way in which it protects them or saves them, much less by
the way it protects or saves itself by them, but by the way in
which it uses and spends them so as to increase them with
"the increase of God."

Thus, in making primary emphasis upon the divine initia-
tive in all our worship and witness, we are not making the
Church's role a purely passive one. God asks of us not a
passive but a willing obedience. He humbles himself that
we might be exalted as "labourers together with him" in
his husbandry and in his building. Just as we rightly reject
all theories of mechanical, verbal inspiration in the prophetic authors of Holy Scripture, so we rightly reject any
ex opere operato doctrine of sacramental grace that dis-
misses as irrelevant to its efficacy the willing response of the
recipients in penitence and faith. So faith itself "cometh by
hearing, and hearing by the word of God." (Romans 10:17)
For

> . . . how shall they believe in him of whom they have
> not heard? and how shall they hear without a preacher?
> and how shall they preach, except they be sent? as it
> is written, How beautiful are the feet of them that
> preach the gospel of peace, and bring glad tidings of
> good things! (Romans 10:14-15)

So God not only desires and seeks, he wills and demands
our active cooperation, risking his designs to the frail conditions of our creaturehood and to our corruption of them
through the pride and selfishness of sin. In this sense, and
in this sense alone, we may say that liturgy and mission are
something that we do with and for God. Isaiah's vision of
worship in the heavenly *Sanctus* was also his call to pro-

phetic witness; his abasement in the confession of his unworthiness was met by his empowering for service. "Woe is
me! for I am undone" was his response to the divine grace;
"Here am I, send me" was his response to the divine summons. That same indissoluble link of worship and mission
is supremely exemplified in Blessed Mary, the archetype of
the Church, both in her unfeigned acceptance of the divine
will and in her responsible acceptance of nurture of the
divine Word made subject to her, that he might increase
"in wisdom and stature and in favor with God and man."
Thus the Church daily in its liturgy, morning and evening,
joins in the thrice-holy *Sanctus* and in the *Magnificat,* that
with all the saints it may be lifted up in adoration and sent
forth in witness.

"GOD IN A BOX"

The liturgy is therefore not an end in itself, even though
it concerns that which is holy and the things which belong
to the world to come. The liturgy is the means in and
through which God acts in his Church to draw all men to
him in Christ. If the Church's *raison d'être* in this world
is to be Christ's own possession and instrument for bringing
to the world his redeeming and reconciling work, then all
that belongs to the Church must serve this supreme purpose, and this includes the precious treasure of the liturgy.
It must not be set apart, separated, and isolated from the
profane and secular world outside, but must be the channel
through which God works to transfigure and make sacred
his whole creation. However true it is that God is the Object
of all worship in the Church, it is all the more true that he
is first of all the acting Subject in worship. All our praise
and thanksgiving and adoration are but context for our

hearkening to his Word and our obedience to his will. All
our offering is nothing worth except as it is given unre-
servedly for his use.

It is always difficult for the Church to keep this proper
sense of proportion in worship. And the more concerned it
is with the purity and beauty of its liturgy the more dangerous is the temptation to an economy of "playing safe" with
it. Our appropriate sense of inadequacy and unworthiness
concerning the holy thing that is committed into our hands
betrays us all too often into designs to protect God by safe-
guards of canon and rubric, and to manage the Spirit by
language and ceremony that remain static and unyielding.
Liturgies always have a tendency, through our overmuch
caution in revising and experimenting, to become progressively archaic. And a great deal of so-called liturgical renewal, if it is not closely watched, gives greater energy to
refurbishing traditions than to wrestling with the problem
of relevance. J. B. Phillips has a terrifying phrase for it:
"God in a box." How much of worship in our churches is
just that! How much devotion is spent in our churches to
keep God, albeit handsomely, even beautifully, maintained
in the box!

All of us who are deeply concerned with the ideals of the
Liturgical Movement must be ever alert to the one test by
which all worship and prayer is laid under judgment,
namely, the sense of mission that they evoke among the
faithful. We must be humbly sensitive to the opposition
and criticism of those who fear preoccupation with liturgical
forms and ceremonies as a perilous accumulation of external
legalisms, gimmicks that both manipulate people to con-
form to church-ways and then deceive them into reckless

attempts to manipulate God. There is a danger, too, of divisive tactics over arbitrary standards of correct or incorrect ways of doing the liturgy, through an incapacity to distinguish the essential from the unessential. I for one could not possibly claim with any honesty that I preach the gospel with greater power by wearing a fourth century alb and chasuble or a thirteenth century surplice and hood than does my friend who wears a sixteenth century black gown and bands or my sainted grandfather who wore a nineteenth century frock coat and white tie. Eric James, in his *Prism* pamphlet *The Roots of the Liturgy,* has some caustic comment on such matters of externals. For example, he points out how much of the discussion these days about the position of the priest at the altar misses the real issue— not the position of the celebrant alone, but of the whole community about the altar, "as though the main thing that mattered at a family meal were where dad sits." (p. 15)

Of course, the externals and the ceremonies of worship have educative value, which are all the more potent because they work like all art so insidiously upon the unconscious. There are actions that enhance understanding, and actions that obscure it. But the understanding of a liturgical act may be turned inward upon itself, and not outward to its relevance to Christian living. This problem is the more perilous for us today when so much energy must be consumed in the mere explanation to church members of what is taking place in the liturgy. The result may very well be only to increase the fun of "playing church" and not to deepen a Christian vocation and stewardship in the political, economic, social, and cultural life of the world. A gospel procession is an impressive ceremony that rightly

adds dignity and splendor to the recital of our Lord's
words and deeds. It is far more expressive and intelligible
than a bobbing sidestepping from an "Epistle" to a "Gospel" side of the altar. Of itself, however, a gospel procession
does not guarantee that the worshipers take heed and
hearken the more to the gospel demand. An offertory procession undoubtedly promotes a larger sense of participation in the act of worship on the part of the laity. Of itself,
it does not increase their missionary giving or witness.

Dr. Geddes MacGregor has recently called attention to
another dimension of the problem of liturgical renewal in
his forthright book, *The Coming Reformation* (Philadel-
phia: Westminster Press, 1960), when he reminds us that
without comparable efforts to deepen personal spirituality
and to reform church discipline, "all attempts at liturgical
revival generally do little more than turn a spotlight on
the interior emptiness of the worshipers." (p. 123) But again,
our notions of true spirituality and of discipline may be
distorted by arbitrary resorts to traditions.

Not long ago I was called down by a devout member of
one of our Catholic parishes so-called, where I had been
supplying during an interim between rectors, for what was
termed my irreverence in communicating people at the late
high Mass. But I cannot honestly believe that self-denial in
a simple Sunday morning breakfast overrides the discipline
of the fullest participation in the sacrificial act of self-giving
in communion. And certainly no act of personal self-denial,
even when performed out of reverence towards God, can
possibly honor him if it does not increase charity towards
the brethren for whom Christ died.

Again, at a recent conference on worship with some of
the women in my diocese, I was asked to recommend some

helpful means of preparation for Holy Communion. Now there are a number of possibilities in answering that question—above all an act of self-examination based upon the three demands in the Invitation of the Eucharistic rite itself: namely, penitence, charity, and faith. But even such a self-examination should lead to positive acts of mercy and of mission. Hence, without any desire to be flippant, I suggested that perhaps the best way to prepare for Holy Communion was to take the trouble and inconvenience of bringing someone else to the service, particularly one who might otherwise be physically handicapped from attendance. There are many empty seats in the cars that Episcopalians drive to church on Sunday morning—quite as many as there sometimes are in the church building itself.

Our concern about the liturgy and so many of the traditional usages associated with it betrays the same kind of mentality that produced in past generations what was called the "mission compound." As converts were won, their lives became more and more involved in the activities and life within the safe walls of the compound. And the change in religion made them lose their identity, and the capacity of communication with their own people and culture. It was not unknown for the converts to be clothed in the missionaries' everyday garments as well as in their liturgical vestments. A hilarious parody of this irrelevance was related to me in the Philippines of the little Igorot girl who appeared in church stark naked except for a cover over her head. One wonders what would have been the scandal to some American churchmen if she had come to church in a dress such as she never wore at home or in the village but with her head uncovered!

The indigenization of worship remains one of the large

problems bequeathed to the leadership of our brother
Churches of Asia and Africa, now that the Western missionaries must of necessity abandon their compounds. But
the "mission compound" mentality is by no means unknown among ourselves. For it is always to be found where
worship is made, however subtly, an escape from mission
and evangelism. A close look at some of the lively issues of
liturgical revival may be disturbing.

Let us begin with what is commonly called "The Parish
Communion," since it has become a *sine qua non* test for
all of us promoters of the Liturgical Movement—and, in
our opinion, rightly so. We shall not stop to argue here the
centrality of the Eucharist, and its proper place as the
normative Sunday worship of Christian congregations. But
what do we mean when we use the word "parish" to modify
the word "Eucharist"? What does "parish" mean to the
average church-goer, even the average Episcopalian church-
goer? Does it refer to a denominational or a sectarian con-
clave? Worse still, does it refer to a particular way of conducting divine worship—say at 9:00 or 9:30 A.M. on Sunday
morning—as distinct from other types of divine service in
the church, or even to other ways of celebrating the Eucharist, whether at 8:00 A.M. or 11:00 A.M.? This is a reckless
way of using great Christian words such as "parish," a way
that denudes them of all relevant meaning. Originally, of
course, "parish" was the word for a "diocese"—for the
whole sphere of Christian corporate life and witness within
a given area. "Parish" is the Christian word for "community"—the community that embraces the believer and the
nonbeliever, the saved and the unsaved. It is the totality of
the people when viewed from the perspective of Christian
possibilities and expectations.

There is, too, a kind of rudeness towards other Christian fellowships in the way some Episcopalians unchurch them from the "parish." But it is even less gracious to find Episcopalian "parishes" in the same neighborhood competing one against another for purely institutional ends. It is utterly disastrous when a single parish divides its own congregation among those who attend "The Parish Eucharist" and those who worship at some other service. If we must change the meaning of the word "parish" let us at least follow the example of the great John Wesley in affirming: "The world is my parish." There are words that belong to ecclesiastical vocabulary that need to be secularized. The Reverend David Paton, in his recent article in *Parish and People* (No. 34, pp. 7-8), has remarked on our semantic failure by asking whether our use of "parish" is not in part responsible for "the difficulty of getting most congregations to take seriously anything that does not happen either in the Church or in the Church Hall." Or conversely, I recall the shock some of my own parishioners had in a former parish when we allowed the use of the church premises for polling booths in a national and state election. They were not mollified at this profanation of the holy place until they were told that we received a small fee for our services—a sum of money that they assumed, of course, would be spent for purely "Church" purposes. So only can some churchmen make friends of the "mammon of unrighteousness."

The whole area of Church-community relations is a touchstone by which liturgy and mission are to be judged. It is not a new problem. Each generation has had its peculiar form of the problem since apostolic times. In our time it is crucial in the area of race relations as has not been the

case since the tensions of Jewish-Gentile differences plagued
the very princes of the apostles. The fact is that the freedom, the hope, and the maturity of so many of the non-
white peoples both of our own and of other lands are so
vastly different today from what they were even two generations ago. And this new situation is in large degree the
blessing of God made evident upon the century-long sacrifice and zeal of Christian mission, of Christian prayer, and
of Christian humanitarian effort. It is not just politics alone
that has brought to fruition within the past decade four
new self-governing provinces of the Anglican Communion
on the continent of Africa. It is not just politics alone that
has seen in our own communion within the past decade
the first national Anglican episcopate in Jordan and Iran,
in the Philippines, and in Cuba; and if we extend our
limits back for another twenty-five or thirty years, we could
add the first national bishops in India and Ceylon, Japan,
Mexico, Brazil, among the Maoris of New Zealand, and
among many of the tribal peoples of Africa. And what we
have said of the Anglican Communion could be said com-
parably of all the other great Churches of the Western,
European-American, world. There is no chapter like it in all
the annals of the Church's history. The present Archbishop
of Canterbury was not exaggerating the promise when he
remarked after the World Council Assembly in New Delhi
that "From now on Christendom is going to be able to
present itself to the world as something which is as much
Asiatic as European."

IS CHRIST DIVIDED—RACIALLY?

Yet in the face of this most exciting of all Christian facts
in our time, there remain innumerable congregations of

Christians in our own beloved Church, of whom it can be
said without contradiction that the presence in their worship of a "heathen and a publican" is more welcome, provided he is white (and such should, of course, be welcome)
than is the presence of a fellow baptized Christian of a
certain race. Yet many of these same congregations give
generously to the Church's quota for mission work among
the colored peoples, and they may even sing with gusto
(provided the tune is familiar) such lines of their hymns as

> In Christ all races meet,
> Their ancient feuds forgetting,
> The whole round world complete,
> From sunrise to its setting. . . .

No matter how we try to rationalize this paradox by
resort to historical, sociological, or psychological explana-
tions, the irrefutable existence of this condition in the
Church is not only a denial of the gospel, it is a blasphemy
against the Holy Spirit. It is a mockery of the holy liturgy
for it rejects the divine grace that works in us to make us
one Body and one Blood in the Lord. It is equally inde-
fensible—and this also is true in many congregations—to
admit churchmen of other races to the Sacrament and then
deny the reality of that Sacrament by refusal to eat and
drink with them in social and professional gatherings, even
in the so-called agapes or suppers of our churches. I can
never erase from my conscience the searching remark of
a fellow priest concerning a particular congregation which
had received in their assembly for Eucharist a fellow African
churchman, but revoked during the time of his attendance
among them the post-Communion coffee hour. "They gave
up," said my friend, "the sacrament that really meant something to them."

No liturgical movement, no restatement of sacramental
theology, that does not face this issue decisively and un-
equivocally can hope to escape the terrible judgment of
God. We must take our stand, as St. Paul took his, from
Jerusalem to Rome, for the equality and liberty of all
Christians at the one table of the one Lord, irrespective of
their race or condition. If we do not, we shall surely pass,
as did Judaizing Christianity, into a ghetto of our own making and finally into historical oblivion.

IS CHRIST DIVIDED—DENOMINATIONALLY?

The ambiguities of Western Christendom in race relations
are not the only obstacles to an effective mission throughout the world. (See Dr. Myers' comments on the one Church,
Chapter VI.) The problem is compounded by the disunity
of the Church. So long as the European and North American Churches enjoyed political and military protection for
their direction of "foreign missions," they could maintain,
even if they could not justify, their competitive enterprise
for converts. But to continue this divisive witness any longer
in Africa or Asia, or even in Latin America, is nothing less
than irresponsible. Rivalry among Christian groups whose
differences are largely accidents of past generations is
meaningless enough; but the continuance of active prosely-
tism among the Christian missions themselves may well be
disastrous. Latin America may very well revert to paganism
unless Roman Catholics and Protestants find a way to cooperation with their present meager resources. Already in
Africa, there are ominous signs that the Christian missions,
handicapped as they are by association with the white man's
imperialism, may by their very divisions which we have
transplanted prove unequal to the attraction of Islam. In

Asia, reunion schemes have made greater progress in the past two decades than they have in any other part of the world, sometimes under the pressure of non-Christian governments. But the peril of Christianity in the face of resurgent Asian nationalisms can only be appreciated if we take seriously to heart the bare statistics: namely, that with the exception of the Philippines, the total number of all professing Christians in the Asian countries adds up to a bare fraction of the total population.

At the present time, the situation is still open and fluid enough to warn us against rash predictions. We know that God is able to use the weak things of the world to confound the mighty. At best we can hope and pray that the newer Churches will rise up to show their mother Churches the way to unity. Whatever our misgivings, we must support them and trust them in the endeavor. For we must admit that we are ourselves impotent in guiding them by our example. In our own land, so long as the Churches have millions to spend on their own institutional maintenance, one despairs of significant achievements of unity. There is little sign among us of a deep penitence for the sin of schism, little indication of passionate longing for reconciliation among separated brethren.

Even in the one agency where Christians of different traditions may meet and work together, the figures of participation are sobering. If we except the Roman Catholic Church, which alone claims one-third of the total Christian membership of the United States, we are left with the fact that the number of Christians included among the member Churches of the National Council of Churches is considerably less than the number in those Churches that remain outside. We in the Episcopal Church know something of the strains created by our own grudging participation in this federation of Churches. Our Lutheran brethren recently experienced a similar searching of soul about their participation. It is not because any of our precious doctrines or forms of worship are imperiled by our membership, but because the leadership of the National Council of Churches has tried to take seriously the relevance of Christian commitment to the broader issues of our common political and social life. We use credal orthodoxy as a camouflage to hide our distaste for prophetic witness.

No one expects all members of any one Church, much less of various and sundry Churches, to be always in agreement concerning the concrete ways and means by which the Christian ethic should be applied to the complicated questions of our national and international concerns. What is disquieting is the refusal of so many Church people to acknowledge the principle that what is proclaimed in worship has also a bearing on what is taking place in the market place. Within the boundaries of a common sacramental fellowship, the tensions and disagreements over the ethical dimensions of political, social, and cultural issues can be borne and transcended, for at the one altar of our common offering and communion the forgiveness of God awaits our repentance and his grace overrules to knit us together in one discipline of forbearance and charity. But where there is no inter-communion, there is less likelihood of such reconciliation, and our old enemy, the devil, takes comfort in using to his own purposes the divided counsels of divided Christians.

The real weakness of the National Council of Churches is not in any threat which it offers to the doctrinal integrity

of its member Churches. Quite the contrary, its abnegation
of all responsibility for questions of "faith and order"
undercuts its power to deal effectively with questions of
"life and work." Without unity in faith, Christians are not
very convincing about their unity in love. Hence the judg-
ments on ethical issues that emanate from a mere federation, without power of discipline and without authority of
doctrine, sound secular, and seem indistinguishable from
the enlightened conscience of humanitarian non-Christians.
Thus, in the racial conflicts of our land, to take an obvious
example, the state through its courts and police power acts
more responsibly than do the Churches to remove inequali-
ties and injustices. And many Church leaders are satisfied
to support the state solely on the basis of the state's own
principle of obedience to law, and neglect the higher Christian teaching of reconciliation for the love of Christ. Let
us not despise justice. God forbid! But let us not forget
love.

REUNION AND LITURGICAL REVIVAL

What then is the role of liturgical revival in this most
baffling problem of Christian reunion? First, let it be said
in all fairness that the modern Liturgical Movement has
already accomplished much amongst the Churches in clearing the air of misunderstandings and prejudice. The Liturgical Movement is one of the brighter hopes on the ecumenical horizon. But its achievements to date have resulted
chiefly from a humble and honest inter-confessional study
of comparative liturgiology. This is not enough, even
though it may induce the Roman Catholics to use the
vernacular, simplify the rubrics, and eliminate peripheral

devotions, or persuade the Protestants to build altars, keep
the Christian year, and adopt at least some guarded sacrificial language in their public prayers.

There can be a delusion in this kind of approach to unity
through liturgical worship. One does not go forward merely
by going backward, however desirable it may be to recover
lost treasures of tradition or to revise distorted emphases
left by the accidents of history. Recovery places us only at
a starting point, not in a position of advance. And what is
the norm of our starting point? We cannot go back to the
Reformation. The best liturgiologists in all the reformed
Churches now know that the sixteenth century Reformers
were very inadequately informed about the principles of
that primitive liturgy which they sought to re-create. We
cannot go back to the undivided Church of the great
patristic age. Our perceptive liturgical friends of the Orthodox Church, which has preserved more intact the patristic
liturgy than any other Church, remind us that the Byzantine
style of worship is hardly fitted for relevance to the twentieth century. So we must go back to the New Testament.
And what do we find? A Church that was eminently liturgical, but one that had no Missal or Prayer Book, no service
manual but the Old Testament, and no defined liturgical
norms other than a living oral tradition, and an obedience
to the Holy Spirit.

The fact is that no one desires or wants liturgical uni-
formity in a reunited Church, least of all one that is a
mere amalgam of the several traditions of our present
divided and defective communions. In all the classic liturgical Churches, the trend is to encourage liturgical diversity
and the indigenous adaptation of inherited rites to native
culture and custom. If we could ever rid ourselves of the

concept of liturgy as a complex of externals, we would even
now be more ready to see the basic similarity that already
exists in the liturgies of all the historic communions: Orthodox, Roman, Anglican, Lutheran, Presbyterian, and Methodist. Each one has its own strengths and its own weak-
nesses. Comparative liturgiology, reinforced by Biblical
theology, has worked wonders in the past twenty-five years
or so in opening a new appreciation of one another's liturgies. There are, of course, certain differences among
them of theological importance—notably their expression
or lack of expression of sacrificial concepts. But the theologians in all communions are making progress towards a
more irenic resolution of the meaning of sacrifice. Dr. Eric
Mascall's comparative studies of this theme in certain leading contemporary theologians of Catholicism and Protes-
tantism gives promise of an exciting breakthrough in this
age-long barrier.

In point of fact, our liturgies are richer and more authentically Biblical and Christian than our textbook sys-
tematic theologies. Dr. Horton Davies is making this judgment with telling effect in his magisterial work on *Worship
and Theology in England,* now in course of publication.
Again and again he shows how devout worshipers in all
Churches grasp in their participation in the sacraments a
true sense of mystery and of the real presence of the Lord
such as one would never suspect from reading the rational-
istic and didactic teaching of their theologians. We who are
Anglicans can testify that the liturgy brings us much nearer
to the heart of religion than all our dogmatic treatises put
together. I suspect the same is true in other Churches. We
can all join in Aquinas' hymns and prayers for Corpus
Christi, when we cannot accept the cool analysis and defini-

tion of his *Summa*. And who would exchange Wesley's
hymns on the Eucharist for all the Methodist treatises on
sacramental theology?

> We need not now go up to heaven
>> To bring the long-sought Saviour down;
> Thou art to all already given,
>> Thou does e'en now thy banquet crown:
> To every faithful soul appear,
>> And show thy real presence here.

So prayed Charles Wesley. And where will you find this
prayer? Not in the Episcopalian or the Methodist hymnals,
but in the Service Book and Hymnal of the Lutheran
Church in America!

If Christians prayed and sang together more, they would
find a more earnest longing for unity. It is not enough to
pray for one another; we must pray with one another. Is
then inter-communion the way to our goal and not merely
the goal itself? Must inter-communion be the term rather
than the instrument of our long and arduous work and
expenditure in the Ecumenical Movement? Cannot God in
his sacramental grace reconcile us more nearly and more
swiftly than we can do in protracted discussion and conference, in reasonable and persuasive argument?

These are not simple questions; and we find diverse answers to them from responsible leaders in many of the
separated Churches. For us who are Anglicans, the very
word "inter-communion" makes us wince; it hits a sensitive
nerve. All the strains and stresses of our boasted compre-
hensiveness meet at this focus of decision. Liturgical considerations alone will not answer our dilemma, for it poses
also canonical and dogmatic issues of momentous significance. The unsophisticated layman who finds no problem

here—"It is the Lord's Table, not ours; why should we not
be charitable? Does it make any real difference to our
Lord?"—should be commended for his sound instincts of
Christian brotherhood. But he should also be warned of
the sin of trifling with God, as though an indiscriminate
inter-communion without grappling with the separated, denominational, and sectarian competitiveness made no difference to our Lord's will that we should be one. Privilege
always carries with it responsibility. There is no quarrel
with a Christian who practices inter-communion and at the
same time subjects himself to the full discipline and stewardship required by each Church in and with which he communicates. But very few of us manage to live up to the
discipline of one Church, much less several.

On the other hand, there is developing a new approach
to the problem that may well be pursued with fruitfulness
—and that is the proposal that Churches which have engaged themselves with utmost seriousness before God to find
a unity at whatever cost of discipline and sacrifice might
engage in authorized acts of inter-communion as a means
of bringing that unity more nearly to accomplishment. This
is a proposal, be it understood, that looks towards a real
organic unity, not an inter-communion between Churches
that continue to exist side by side as mutually recognized
entities in the same place of witness. There are, of course,
many hazards to a Church making this kind of resolution.
It demands a depth of faith and penitence, and of willing
obedience to the Spirit that we must confess seems far removed from the complacency and self-satisfaction now ex-
hibited by so many Churches—not least, we very proud
Anglicans. But it is worth recalling from time to time the
bold promise of our bishops in the Lambeth Conference of

1948 that a united Church, truly Catholic and Evangelical, cannot be "in the limiting sense of the word Anglican." It must be "something more comprehensive," by which they meant, I trust, a Church more fully Christian.

AUTHENTICALLY CHRISTIAN WORSHIP

The liturgical revival can contribute to this great end by a primary concern with an authentically Christian worship in all the Churches that is neither iconoclastic towards the past nor irrelevant to the here and now. Such worship today calls for great affirmations—affirmations about God and about the world from the perspective of God's designs and promises. It calls for a liturgy that affirms the goodness of God in his whole creation, that rids men of all "taboos" as it does of all selfish indulgence in the material things that God has made, that delivers them from the torment of dread of destruction and annihilation. Such a liturgy takes seriously the scriptural injunction "to make prayers and supplications, and to give thanks for all men." An authentically Christian worship affirms the universality of Christ's redemption, the earnest of our dignity and liberty and freedom in the perfect Son of Man, and the source of all power to overcome selfishness and sin and whatever "evils which the craft and subtilty of the devil or man worketh against us." Such a liturgy must offer a real hope of spiritual renewal, by transfiguring the patterns of human relations and evoking creative acts of love and unfeigned generosity. It must "knit together in one communion and fellowship" every sort and condition of mankind. The adventure of liturgical renewal is the adventure of realizing what it means to be a living member of Christ's one Holy Catholic Church at all times and in all places, and the adventure for each and every one of us of confessing Jesus Christ as our personal Lord and Saviour. By such affirmations, worship is witness, and liturgy is mission.

> Little children, let us not love in word or speech but in deed and in truth. By this we shall know that we are of the truth, and reassure our hearts before him whenever our hearts condemn us; for God is greater than our hearts, and he knows everything. (I John 3:18-20 RSV)

CHAPTER II

THE LITURGICAL MOVEMENT IN THE ROMAN CATHOLIC CHURCH

by

Joseph T. Nolan

The Wichita Liturgical Conference met at the same time as another great assembly, the Second Vatican Council, in Rome. The Second Vatican Council invited and rejoiced in the presence of brethren from other faiths. At Wichita, Bishop Carroll, Monsignor Fischer, the late Father Ellard, S.J., and I responded to that same generous spirit on the part of the Associated Parishes—that unity in charity which is so important.

When we consider how difficult it is to convey the right ideas on subjects like liturgy, episcopacy, sacraments, to our other Christian brethren, we Roman Catholics feel a special kinship to the Anglican Communion. In the earthly mansions of our Father's house, we think of our Anglican and our Orthodox brethren as our closest neighbors; we live, so to speak, on the same street. The Wichita Conference had invited me to be more than an observer. I had been invited to be a participant and, again like the Vatican

Council at that very moment, to take up the subject of the
sacred liturgy.

The great action of the liturgy is, of course, the Eucharistic Sacrifice. St. Augustine and others have often suggested the ways in which the Eucharist serves as a sign of
unity: the myriad kernels and the many grapes, united by
so much human activity into single substances, the bread
and the wine. Indeed they are symbols of ourselves, come
from far and wide, assembled by so much laborious human
activity (hard-working committees, for example) into one
great assembly, with one noble purpose. This is the unity
of moral purpose. But we seek something deeper: the unity
of sacramental life. The Eucharistic bread and wine, by
the power of the Holy Spirit, become nothing less than the
Body and Blood of Christ. The Spirit breathes where he
wills, and no man knows of his coming or going. But by
the power of that same Spirit, we pray it may come to pass
that we be united still more: into one body, the Body of
Christ.

Through Baptism we already share more than a common
purpose; we share a common supernatural life. In address-
ing the members of the Wichita Conference as my fathers
and brothers and sisters in Christ, I was stating a splendid
reality and calling to mind an unfinished mission—that all
things are to be, one day, *in Christ,* "until there is only one
Christ, praising and adoring the Father."

If we address ourselves specifically to the Liturgical Movement in the Roman Catholic Church, we fortunately can
conclude that it is a genuine movement—no mere theory,
or scholarly thesis, or scheme of rubrics. At times it was
even thought by some to be a sort of underground movement, and I must admit that its pioneer spirits feel a sort of

kinship with the survivors of the Long March in China, or the "old Bolsheviks" of the Russian Revolution—we, too, have survived! And we have seen this interest become a mighty tide of spiritual renewal, what Pope Pius XII called a providential work of the Holy Spirit, a springtime in the life of the Church.

In this chapter we shall look first at its historical background; then, its present status in America. We shall note such features as the surprising development of participation in worship, the not surprising development of many problems of inertia and resistance; and finally, the significance of the movement for our times.

Illustrating two attitudes towards the liturgy is the true-life incident of a young naval lieutenant from Boston returning from the Pacific in World War II. He was coming out of a large Catholic Church in Milwaukee on a Saturday evening and inquired if on the next day, Sunday, there was to be a high Mass. The reply of the sexton was a sort of classic. "There is," he admitted, "but it doesn't take any longer than the others. They have a fast priest!" It needs only to be added that the young lieutenant in question did not end up in the White House. He ended up in Galena, Kansas, and is writing this chapter.

Now, to answer the question, "What is the Liturgical Movement?" it would be too simple to depend on that story. It really is not a movement by high Mass enthusiasts to have their way and to educate or extirpate others like the poor sexton who choose the low road instead of the high and who may well get to Scotland or Heaven before us! And yet, the attitude that considers the liturgy something to do and get over with, helps us to appreciate the problem.

HISTORY OF THE LITURGICAL MOVEMENT

In the first six centuries of the Church the liturgy was the principal school of Christian formation. That it was successful is borne out by the astounding fact that without the aid of a single mimeograph machine, the Church converted the Roman Empire! Lest praise of this "classic period" of liturgy seem too fanciful, we can refer to the sober works of the greatest Catholic scholar on the Mass, Father Jungmann.[1]

In our own day the liturgy is still a school of Christian living, and we are all enrolled in this school, so to speak, by our Baptism. But nowadays a good many of us don't understand the course! The liturgy is the official worship of the whole Church: Christ the Head and we the members; for us, of course, it is expressed principally in the holy sacrifice of the Mass. But the work of Christ is continued in his sacraments; the sacrifice of praise we call the Divine Office goes on before and after the Mass, throughout the day, and the teaching and redeeming acts of Christ are renewed through the celebration of the liturgical year. This is liturgy, official public worship and cult, the center of all sanctity.

But these, especially the Mass, were the areas increasingly separated from the people until the liturgy eventually came to be thought of and carried out as a specialized activity of the clergy, on the one hand, resulting in a sort of spiritual benefice for the laity, on the other. Increasingly the laity became passive recipients, not active participants, and liturgy from the Middle Ages to our own day became more

[1] Joseph A. Jungmann, S.J., *The Mass of the Roman Rite* (New York: Benziger Brothers, 1959), for example.

of a performance than a family affair. The holiness of the
Roman Christian at the time of Gregory the Great and of
the medieval Christian at the time of Gregory VII are both
from the liturgy; they must be, for it is the redeeming and
sanctifying acts of Christ extended through time. But the
former was more direct, through forms of outward participation that led to an inner identity as God's holy people; the latter was more indirect, like people who come in
after the banquet and are fed the same food, served in a
different fashion at another table.

How did a movement of restoration come about within
our own Church? It came from the monasteries, where happily it did not confine itself; from Benedictines, who did
not keep it as their own special preserve. The first of the
monks one should mention is Dom Prosper Gueranger
(1832), who sought to explain the riches of the liturgical
year. He pioneered, but did not rise above a conception of
the liturgy as akin to a gorgeous court ceremonial. And
when this view prevails, as it did in the seventeenth to
nineteenth centuries, the liturgy is embellished until it
finally is all but embalmed. That is when you have the
condition that Father Shepherd refers to in Chapter I as
"God in a box." Gueranger, however, did create an awareness of the subject at a time when piety was going in ego-
centric ways, and it was his monastery of Solesmes that began the restoration of the Church's most authentic religious
music, the Gregorian chant. The restoration has been so
successful that today it presents us with a major problem,
and source of opposition, in questions of the high Mass, the
vernacular, and the chant.

The German theologians of the nineteenth century, like
Scheeben, were other pioneers, reaching as far back as St.

Cyril of Alexandria and anticipating Pope Pius XII, in
representing the Church as the Mystical Body of Christ.
Not a building, but a body. Or if a building, built up of
living stones, a temple of the Lord. No doctrine is richer
or more fundamental to this whole reform.

And now it thrills the heart to mention one of the greatest
of the Belgians, Dom Lambert Beauduin and his Abbey of
Mont Cesar. He was a man of great practical wisdom who
came from the secular priesthood and a ministry to laboring
people, to the conviction that his ideals of social justice
could only be achieved by renewing the true liturgical
spirit. He gave his life to help this movement embrace the
humble man, the laboring man, and finally, the Christian
of other faiths.

Next is the great German Abbot, Ildefons Herwegen, who
emphasized the unity of the *Church* with God. Spiritual
writers had oriented their thinking around the union of
the *soul* with God, giving rise to the question of objective
and subjective piety, which became a burning issue and
a needless dichotomy that was finally removed by the su-
perbly balanced view of Pius XII in his encyclical on the
sacred liturgy, *Mediator Dei*. It was Abbot Ildefons who
made the Abbey of Maria Laach a center of liturgical
studies and profoundly experienced worship. Father Hans
Reinhold, the most valuable pastor-author, was a student
there in 1921, and gives us the following description of a
turning point in Maria Laach's revolution:

> One beautiful afternoon the seven mighty bells of our
> old minster rang, and a limousine drove up to the
> gates. In it was the Cardinal Archbishop of Cologne.
> Apparently "headquarters" had asked him to look into
> the matter and to find out what sort of "mysteria" the

monks and their guests were performing. Well, the result of this visit was that next morning a certain member of the sacred college had tears in his eyes, and
that a year later he stood behind a portable altar in
his own huge cathedral saying the Missa Recitata with
the whole congregation.

The other great monk of Maria Laach was Dom Odo
Casel.[2] At the very least, his *mysterium* theory aided the
realization that the liturgical year is not a mere anniversary
service. There were other Germans, not monks but theologians whose graceful minds are still with us: Karl Adam,
and he whom Italy and Germany can both claim, Romano
Guardini.[3]

So much depends on emphasis, and they helped to restore
the balance. "What think ye of Christ" is not only the basic
test of any Christian but a determinant for the shape of
the liturgy and the piety of the faithful. He is God, and
the emphasis on his divinity can be glorious—and was very
necessary, after Arianism. But the tendency followed to be
overawed by his divinity, and to make the liturgy a glorious
spectacle, the descent of God among men.

But we know that Christ is not only God but the God-
Man, and remember that St. Paul said every high priest is
taken from among men. And this is the Christ who truly
said, "The Spirit of the Lord is upon me." That full anoint-
ing of the Spirit makes the God-Man our one great High
Priest who has entered the holy of holies forever. If we
emphasize Christ as man, never denying his divinity but
trying to see in his humanity the full scope of divine pur-

[2] Odo Casel, *The Mystery of Christian Worship* (Westminster, Md.:
Newman Press, 1962).

[3] Romano Guardini, *The Spirit of the Liturgy* (New York: Sheed
& Ward, 1955).

pose, then we realize his nearness to us, that he is the elder
brother of all mankind, first-born of every creature, even of
the dead. Humanity is on its way to God. Yes, but *with*
God, for he said, "I am the way." (John 14:6)

How much it really means to say the great doxology: *"per
ipsum, et cum ipso, et in ipso!"* "In him" might well remind us of him who is divine and shares divine life with
us, so that we are incorporated in him. "With him" is the
beautiful image of Christ the Good Shepherd, who called
us his friends and taught us to pray *"our* Father." "Through
him" is the great work of Christ the Mediator who has
opened the heavens for us but has neither left us nor forgotten us: the great High Priest who every day gathers our
oblations into the mighty chalice of his eternal sacrifice.

Is all this too deep for the average man? Not when these
themes were expressed as pastoral liturgy by the Austrian
monk with a parish, Pius Parsch, and again with Dom
Lambert and his popular magazine and missal, and the
energetic Belgians who introduced the form of dialogue
Mass. How did the movement cross the seas? There was
another Benedictine, Dom Virgil Michel, a Thomist and
sociologist, a true Christian humanist and far-reaching
pioneer. He founded the liturgical review *Orate Fratres;*
in thirty-four years it has had only one other editor, the
excellent Father Godfrey Diekmann.

Incidentally, his problems in changing the magazine's
name throw some light on Catholic attitudes. He finally
agreed the magazine needed a vernacular title when he
learned that the freight office personnel referred to it as
"O-rayt freights." In a contest three people turned up the
prize-winning title, which was *Worship*—and the objection

was promptly made by some that this sounded too Protestant!

Among the American pioneers I would single out my own dear friend and father in the Lord, Monsignor Martin B. Hellriegel. When they ask him how long he has been in the Liturgical Movement he answers, "Since my Baptism." He has, in St. Louis, what may truly be called a living parish, and has taught many of us the secrets of the more abundant life. And then there is a most unusual man, a Kansan, no less, but unusual because a prophet vindicated, a prophet *with* honor. I refer to the late Father Gerald Ellard, who was happily among us at Wichita. He got in this movement, too, with his Baptism, but he spent fifty years of it as a Jesuit, and this was a singular grace indeed. Father Ellard was not only a true scholar of the liturgy, but he was so imbued with its spirit that he would always share his notes and files, a treasure-trove indeed. If someone asked just what is meant by Christian life and worship, whether it could be summed up in a few words, I could say in St. Augustine's two words: "in Christ"—or I could sum up "Christian Life and Worship," not in a few words, but in Father Ellard's great textbook by that title.

There were many more who were eager to sing the song of the Lord in a strange land. In our time the man with the greatest influence by way of doctrine and direction was Pope Pius XII. His predecessors did much. St. Pius X at the turn of the century emphasized that music is the handmaid, not the master of the liturgy, and it was he who began the right stress on the Holy Eucharist. Pius XI suggested that we do not pray *at* Mass but rather *pray the Mass,* and it was he who underlined the potential of the liturgical year

to teach doctrinal truths so effectively because it reaches
the whole man, and often, with a variety that should never
tire. Pius XII did so very much. Early in his pontificate he
gave a definition of the Mystical Body and later a complete
encyclical and extended definition of the liturgy. He extended reforms to the Breviary, Holy Week, the Church
calendar, granted the vernacular rituals, and finally gave
us two great charters for liturgical renewal: the first in 1955
for the musical part of worship, and the second, in 1958, his
death-bed testament, for the people's part in worship. No
longer were they to be "mute and silent spectators" or, in
Pope John's more pointed phrase, "like so many telephone
poles." It is of great significance, and certainly of divine
providence, that this pope with no pastoral background,
consumed with problems of war and peace and the relevance
of the Church to a scientific age, is the same man who said
(and acted upon his own words): "A Christian's chief duty
and supreme dignity is to participate in the Eucharistic
Sacrifice, and to increase and nourish its supernatural
spirit."

STATUS OF THE LITURGICAL MOVEMENT

What of liturgical activity at present among Catholics in America? The Liturgical Weeks, similar to the
Anglican Liturgical Conference in Wichita, are now round-
ing out a quarter century. The movement is not only very
much "above ground" and in the sunlight, but also in the
spotlight; there were no less than eleven hundred priests
and three to four thousand of the laity at the Notre Dame
Liturgical Week. These study weeks are sponsored by a
Liturgical Conference of priests, sisters, and laity who have
deeply loved and sacrificed for the apostolate of liturgy

these many years and who now find themselves on the
borders, at least, of the promised land. There are new
centers of liturgical study, such as Notre Dame, which
produce such remarkable books as Father Bouyer's *Liturgical Piety*. There are diocesan commissions of liturgy; these
always have been, but they are active now and developing
programs of participation. And this has become the key
word! Everywhere we are teaching why and how we should
participate in worship—why we should change from Masses
with silent congregations, from habits of individual piety,
to spoken and sung prayer, procession, involvement. And
how we can express our worship *ex*ternally, through vernacular prayer and song, through Latin responses directly
with the celebrant, through restoring the ordinary chants of
high Mass to the faithful, through some expression of offering as well as receiving at Mass—offering the altar breads
as token of offering ourselves. We now teach these external
forms so we can deepen thereby our part in worship *in*-
ternally, "putting on the mind that is in Christ Jesus." We
urge upon all this program for three reasons.

Psychological: Man is not an angel. Sense and sound
have their humble roles to play in leading him to con-
templation.

Social: Man is not an atom, an atomized individual, but
a person, and a social person. He is part of a family, in this
case God's own.

Doctrinal and Sacramental: We take part because we are
a part, members of the Body whose head is Christ, sharing
in his priesthood by the sacramental characters of Baptism

and Confirmation. Once again, this takes explanation and
a shift of emphasis. For too long we have thought of Baptism
only as an escape from original sin, and Confirmation only
as making us soldiers. The other idea, of participation in
Christ's priesthood, is equally spelled out in St. Thomas.
And our precise role as priest is to offer, in our degree, the
sacrifice which the *ordained* priest consecrates and offers.
Our sacrifice is Christ's Body and Blood, which he offered
in a supreme act of love for us and of obedience to the will
of his Father. Our lives must be sacrificial, because we are
incorporated in him, and we accomplish this likewise
through acts of love for each other and obedience to the
will of our Father.

What evidence is there right now of all this doctrine in-
forming practice, giving a new look and sound to Catholic
worship? I would say about 10 per cent of our parishes
have successfully worked out participation in the Mass
through these external forms. Many more have tried it.
Far more widespread is the use of the layman's missal. It is
also increasingly common to see altars built to look like
tables of sacrifice, not shrines or pedestals, and churches
planned to assemble God's people around the altar, to focus
on worship.

There is a new type of Catholic emerging, still very
much a minority, but a minority that can grow to be a
determining number, the leaven in the Mass. He is growing into a program of adult catholicism. At Sunday Mass he
will speak out in bold affirmation of his faith and perhaps
be trained to act as a lector or commentator, to lead others.
He will even sing, as befits a vocation of joy and love, and
he is coming to realize two neglected aspects of worship:
first, that sacrifice calls for offering as well as receiving, and

second, that when we receive Communion, it is not so much receiving it as achieving it—achieving a union in charity with Christ, and through Christ in each other. This gives our adult Christian some new thoughts on work and worship. Where else, except in the world, can he apply the gospel and do the good works that are joined to the great Good Work? And how can he possibly indulge in something like racial prejudice if he is trying to achieve this communion with his brother in Christ? The adult Christian is coming to realize that the Sacraments and the gospels are more the guidelines of the Christian life than the ten commandments; the prayer of the Psalms can be his daily prayer also; and Baptism appears so significant that he might even remember and celebrate the anniversary of the most important day in his life.

The problems we have encountered have to do with human nature at any time and with human society at this particular time. Many people are almost constitutionally opposed to change; their position is akin to that of the Old Timer who had to admit that he had seen many changes in his lifetime, but could at least lay claim to a consistent position: he was against them all! The Catholic Church is far from being a monolith, nor can we feed directives into people like so many punch-cards into an IBM machine and expect the same swift results. When changes in worship are introduced the favorite argument of many is, "We didn't use to do it this way." The irony here is that the early Church *did* do it this way. But the winds of change are blowing. As an example of coordinated effort, using all the skills available for the great act of worship, I think of a Mass I was privileged to celebrate to open the student year at Xavier University in Cincinnati, Ohio. When I arrived

the night before I was told to hurry to the arena because
the teams were practicing. Up to now this has meant the
boys of the football and basketball squads, and it was a
pleasant surprise to find that the teams meant the singers
and servers of Mass. The glee club was, *mirabile dictu,*
using its fine talents not for the usual performance of
Invictus but to lead 1800 students in singing the Good
Shepherd Psalm for a communion song.

A prominent, beautifully arrayed altar had been erected
high in the center of the gym, with students on three sides
as I faced them. They celebrated with me to the fullest
extent in prayer and song. The speech department had
provided the best students to read the Scriptures; a young
physician-alumnus was the skilled commentator; the communion of the vast crowd was accomplished swiftly and
reverently with priests going out to "communion stations";
the students received standing; the song was real prayer.
This is the only time I have seen a university Mass studied
from the angle of the most fruitful participation and prepared as a work of art, not for any aesthetic but for deeply
liturgical reasons; the planners showed a deep respect for
the students' right and capacity to worship.

Also in the same city I studied on Sunday the problem
of the big parish. The biggest parish is St. William's with
five thousand people and twelve Sunday Masses. Monsignor
Robert Sherry, a long-time liturgist and vernacularist, knows
full well that the eventual solution must be smaller parishes.
But now he faces a practical situation by having music at
no less than ten of the Sunday Masses, with prayer, song,
the assistance of four priests; every possible effort is made
to make worship gracious and meaningful. As the organ
sounded throughout the church and the processional cross

passed through the crowded vestibule, I thought that at
least they had a visible reminder that Christ has passed
among us and leads us again. A layman assured me there
was indeed progress; the vestibule crowd no longer stepped
out for a smoke during the sermon! Now, the educated
Catholic knows perfectly well, even when he is on the dim
edge of a silent crowd, that he is on holy ground, that the
great action of the Mass is proceeding, and that it is good
for him to be there. But Monsignor Sherry and other wise
pastors know full well how often attention lags, how thin
instruction may have been, and how much of it anyway
should come by actual participation, a learning-by-doing
which is both good liturgy and good common sense.

SIGNIFICANCE OF THE LITURGICAL MOVEMENT

As for human society at this particular time, it is not
only secular but frantically preoccupied with pursuits of
leisure and work. There is small ability to be silent, to take
the time for worship and meditation, or to use creative
skill. We do not sing, but turn on a machine; we get our
music as well as our food from cans. It is all very well to
talk profoundly of something like the liturgical year, but
what does it mean to the average mixed-up Christian? Probably nothing more than Christmas, and possibly a touch
of Lent. Advent he never heard of, because it is swallowed
up in Christmas which, for him, begins right after Thanksgiving!

The climax of our liturgical year is the Paschal mystery,
and the following example from the green wood points up
our problem of making the liturgy relevant to daily life. In
1947, during the Boston Liturgical Week which explored
in anticipation the theme of a restored Easter Vigil, I

talked as a layman with one of the country's foremost
liturgical artists. It was the time of Cardinal Stepinac's
trial in Yugoslavia, and she told me that in the light of
such excruciating issues as this in the Church it was the
height of some kind of absurdity to have a Catholic conference get all excited about having the Holy Saturday
service at midnight. And, of course, if you consider it just
a candlelight service which is obviously prettier in the darkness, then she is right. But that isn't the point; it isn't Holy
Saturday so much as it is the vigil of Easter and the whole
triumph of our redemption, which the liturgy re-presents so
we can join in. We may know this as priests, but our people
do not know it—not very well anyway—and they often find
the liturgy irrelevant even to the business of being good,
of becoming holy.

All this means we have a massive job of re-education, and
this, too, has been part of our liturgical revival. Here is
an example of how it should work. You know that a scale
model helps us to appreciate a larger reality. Perhaps we
can teach the greatest of all realities if we present the
parallel of *Sunday worship* and the *Paschal mystery* and the
mystery of Christian death. Every week is like a microcosm,
a scale model of the Christian life: the week with its trials
and labor, and then the Sunday in which we offer the fruits
of our labor. Lent and Easter reproduce this on a larger
scale: Lent, during which we engage in a mighty spiritual
effort, and Easter, or rather, the whole Paschal mystery, in
which Christ's redeeming death invites us to die to sin, to
love as he loves (let us not forget that), and to rise up to a
new vigor in the Christian life. Then, finally, we complete
the picture when we realize that the whole of life is like a
Lent, a journeying in the desert towards the promised land.

And it reaches a climax with a death that is uniquely our own but also a share in the Passion, joined to his saving death. So it becomes indeed a "passing over," the death wherein we are born again to that eternal Easter which is the full splendor of the risen life. This is the vision to give our people, to give meaning and purpose to their week, to the years that pass, to the whole of Christian life.

There are several other phases of the liturgical revival in the Roman Catholic Church which would be of particular interest to our fellow Christians. First and most striking is the wonderful new emphasis throughout the Catholic world on music, and this includes the congregational singing of good hymns quite as much as Gregorian chant. Never among the Germans and Poles, but certainly among other Catholic groupings, including the Irish and Americans, we seem to have forgotten St. Augustine's dictum that "singing we pray, and praying we sing." We seem to have forgotten, too, that the description of the very first Mass concludes with the words, "And a hymn being sung, they went out to Mount Olivet." (Matthew 26:30) When Pliny wrote his famous letter to Trajan in 116 A.D., he described Christians as apparently harmless people "who gather before dawn and sing a hymn to Christ as if he were God." I have thought, rather ruefully, how times change, at least with a Catholic congregation. I doubt that we could get them out before dawn, or that they would know a hymn at all.

But times are still changing! Even with dawn: this is the latest hour for celebrating the Easter Vigil and the Mass of the Resurrection in Germany, and as for singing a hymn, at last we are getting over a sort of suspicion that this would turn us into Protestants! The new decrees insist that the hymns be sober, emotionally speaking, reflect good

doctrine and, if used during the Mass action, be appropriate to the structure of the Mass. This has meant that a
good many of the "old favorites" have been taken out and
given a decent Christian burial; it has also meant that some
people have come to consider this Liturgical Movement as
an outrageous business that denies them the hymns that
mother used to sing. In the parishes of the 10 per cent we
mentioned above, you are most likely to find a processional
and recessional hymn now, and in the past ten years the
new favorites are "Praise to the Lord," and the Trinity
hymn, "God, Father, Praise and Glory."

Perhaps it seems almost sentimental to expect great things
from a revival of song, compared to the profound stirrings
in the worlds of Scripture and theology. But I agree with
what Father Shepherd says in Chapter I on this point, and
both of us can summon no less an intellect than St.
Augustine, who testified to the effect of song in the liturgy
at St. Ambrose's cathedral at Milan in bringing him to the
truth. And the psalms that moved Augustine to tears are
being sung again, in tears and laughter, as truly popular
songs: I speak of an astonishing success in France by Father
Gelineau in giving a new mode of singing to vernacular
psalms. They are being sung everywhere, like Christian
folk-songs; I use the English version gladly, and consider
this a major breakthrough.

As the revival of congregational singing in our own
Church continues, I look for, and propose, *a joint hymnal*
with Anglicans and other Christians. At a convention of
the American Guild of Organists, Protestants and Catholics
together sang, "O God of Loveliness," and were thrilled to
realize they had found a way to pray together. I think that

a joint hymnal, as well as a joint Bible translation, would be very much to have in common.

The Liturgical Movement receives some of its strongest support from our missionary bishops, like Bishop Bekkum of Indonesia. These men recognize the importance of not trying to westernize the East; indeed, the Church should know from her early history how to incorporate and elevate a native culture, but too often in recent centuries we have found the Gothic cathedral planted among the pagodas. (See what Father Merchant has to say about this sort of thing in Chapter III.) The vernacular rituals, and even a partially vernacular Mass, have been freely granted in mission lands, and the new approach may include native customs in sacred rites as well as native languages.

The Liturgical Movement has not only become eminently pastoral in our Church, but among liturgical thinkers there is a vital link, a cross-fertilization, with the biblical renewal, the emphasis on preaching, the lay apostolate, works of social justice, and, particularly, the Ecumenical Movement. In regard to this new *entente cordiale* and liturgical interest among Catholics and other Christians we are asked if it comes about because we are now emphasizing Scripture, congregational singing, lay activity, etc. The answer is Yes, but it goes deeper. It seems obvious that as Catholics get more scriptural and Protestants more liturgical, they are bound to meet each other! It is good to know that the Bible is used in Catholic churches and the altar in Protestant ones. But of deeper significance is the fact that we Catholics have been stressing doctrines which others appreciate and think we do not (sometimes they have been right); I refer to the mediatorship of Christ, our share in his priesthood, the importance of Baptism and professing this faith in later years, the necessity of bearing witness in Christian life, especially after Confirmation. Most of all, the Liturgical Movement is an ecumenical force because it is manifestly the work of the Holy Spirit, the Spirit of truth, and as it deepens the life of the Christian, this life which is God's own is increasingly manifest in charity. And love unites.

Perhaps a fitting conclusion to this chapter in a book with the splendid title "Liturgy is Mission," would be to recall the story of a cartoon that made history in the Communist world. It was by the great Finnish cartoonist, Sari; he showed two shop windows, one labeled "Capitalism" and the other, "Communism." The one labeled "Capitalism" was just jammed with consumer goods and luxury goods: the sable and the Cadillac, the deep carpet and the comfortable life. Underneath was the title, "Commodities Without Ideas." The window labeled "Communism" was very Spartan and bare; there were only the portraits of Lenin and Stalin (which would have to be updated now!), the works of Karl Marx, the hammer and sickle, and the dove of peace. Underneath it said, "Ideas Without Commodities."

At this moment in history, when the supreme test is upon us, we are compelled to ask ourselves who will win the allegiance of men: the people who proclaim the ideals of brotherhood, as the Communists do, or the ones so busy with the knobs of their color TV sets. The protest may well be made that we Christians have the correct idea of brotherhood, with God as our Father; the Communists are the deceivers. Yes, but how often we have betrayed our message and turned our words into tinkling cymbals. The arrogant agents of colonialism, of unbridled capitalism, and offensive racism—how often these have been the baptized sons and daughters of the Lord, and how little their Communion has meant, how empty their hands and souls of gifts for the altar!

In these days we are all discussing the sacred liturgy more widely and deeply than ever before. It is the best of all commodities, purchased by the blood of Christ. We have a Liturgical Movement in our churches and a Council right now to give us some new ideas. They are urgently needed. For too long we have kept our liturgy to ourselves; we have often failed to appreciate the Lord's bequest to us in sacrifice and sacrament, or their significance for social reform as well as social worship, or in what sense the Christian is to be Christ in the world. Our spiritual renewal is part, perhaps the most important part, of a supreme effort to renew the face of the earth. We shall succeed, or see the earth destroyed. "The time is coming, and indeed is now here, when we *must* worship the Father in sincerity and truth." (John 4:23)

CHAPTER III

THE CHURCH'S MISSION TO THE ARTIST

by

W. Moelwyn Merchant

It is altogether possible that many people will fear from the title of this chapter that it is concerned with peripheral matters, things that are on the edge—decorative, nice addenda that you needn't pay too much attention to, but that it would still be nice to have if you could afford them.

WORD AND ICON

This attitude to the arts—to what you see and to what you hear in Church—has been one of the pernicious stumbling blocks in the way of an effective ministry in many areas. And yet it should be pointed out that if ours is a sacramental religion (and we have no business speaking with the kind of theology we do if ours is *not* a sacramental religion), then the *word* and the *icon,* that which you hear and that which you see, are vital to our very faith.

Now *word* and *icon* are central for two *kinds* of people:

81

the poet and dramatist on the one side; the painter, the sculptor, and the architect on the other. These are the people professionally engaged with the substance of our missionary activity. These are the people who are the experts, yet the people, on the whole, who are the last to be consulted by us. We leave them on the edge of things.

The artist, however, has the right to ask, "What makes the Church determined to have a special mission to me?" He could say with Shylock, "Have I not eyes? If you do tickle me, do I not laugh?" The artist is a man like the rest of us and if the Church thinks that it has a peculiar mission to the artist, then it may be indulging in a piece of special pleading or of arrogance which is really rather unseemly either way. In fact, it is just possible that for the Church visible (or shall we say that fallen portion of it which is the instrument of the Church, namely we who are its members) the mission is from the artist to the Church, to redeem some of the aspects of our apparently uncreative faith.

If we are truly a visible body on earth, then we have certain obligations to men—not simply as men but in their particular and special vocation. In this sense it may be perfectly true that we do have a mission to the artist, but there is something perhaps a little more delicate that we should exercise towards him. We should in the first place be prepared to give him that which appears to deny the very corporateness of our Church itself—that which the saints have sometimes demanded: total isolation, peace—to work out the implications of his vocation (as Bishop Pike uses the word in Chapter V)

The kind of gathering that most of us enjoy, with its concomitants of hurry, hearty good fellowship, and the sheer pleasure of meeting would probably be anathema to the artist in most of his moods. Very little artistic creativity could go on in the hurry and bustle of the typical parish, diocesan, or even national meeting; and these are, after all, only microcosms of a great deal of the daily work of the Church. We move rather fast for the artist, and the artist wishes to withdraw. Are we willing to give him his peace—allow him to go into his little cell occasionally to work out the implications of his vision? That can sometimes be an embarrassing thing to the Church. The artist can so very frequently see more than one jump ahead of his fellow men. The implications of his mission may take him teetering to the edge of heresy, to a point where a less skillful mortal would topple right over.

By way of example, I vividly recall the occasion on which I had the privilege of beginning what has become a long and very valued friendship with Christopher Fry. I had been asked by the Religious Drama Society to read *A Sleep of Prisoners* to see whether it was theologically sound. I did so with some trepidation lest I should be rushing in where an artistic angel ought to fear to tread. I read the play through very carefully; towards the end, trying to do my work as an "external examiner," I found a phrase that I thought I could quarrel with: "the enterprise is *exploration into God.*" I wrote at once, post haste. I asked Christopher Fry if he really seriously thought that the whole of the Christian faith was exploration into God. Wouldn't it be theologically more acceptable, I asked, if he were prepared to add some such phrase as "God's exploration into us," for was grace not from God to us and was our exploration not a response to that grace? I felt I had expressed my objection quite impeccably. Nevertheless, his reply was:

"It doesn't appear to me to fit the rhythm of the verse at that point!" And then the delightful leg puller added rather more soberly, "I think that you cannot quite expect me to pack into one quite small play the whole impeccability of Christian doctrine."

I withdrew at that point as gracefully as I could, and I am glad to say that we have been firm friends ever since. Had a person in my place been more meddlesome and demanded on behalf of the Church that the phrase be modified (not that it was positively heretical; it was only perhaps a little partial) Fry might very well have withdrawn the play altogether. And that would have been the Church's loss.

It is not enough to talk about the Church's mission to the artist. We must add that the Church must voluntarily be prepared not to limit the artist's vision. Forbearance of this kind gives the artist his peace. Let us not badger him too far. That is something that the Church has not always remembered.

For the Church has the hierarchy, who must be careful in exercising patronage. Sometimes their safety can be most dangerous for the artist—especially if it percolates down into the laity who are exercising an even wider patronage.

At our safe distance from the Renaissance, we may be able to see that Michelangelo's Last Judgment in the Sistine Chapel is not only a piece of marvelous *artistic* integrity and insight, but a piece of *spiritual* insight at the same time. Looking at it somewhat less casually than we do at the post card illustration of it, we may be a little frightened at that menacing gesture of Christ's arm coming down and condemning the doomed to their damnation.

In our nicer twentieth century, we may not quite believe in the damned in the way Michelangelo did; but the Papal Court did not take that kind of objection to the masterpiece. The Pope's master of ceremonies at the time, upon returning from what we could call a private preview, said to the Pope, "It is more fit for a place of debauchery than for the Pope's private chapel." Michelangelo heard of this remark, and he painted the head of that master of ceremonies into one of the figures in Hell. When the master of ceremonies then protested to the Pope and said that this was most unseemly, the Pope answered in these delicious terms, "What a pity—I could have *done* something if he had put you in Purgatory!"

But that is not by any means the most recent example of the way in which we are meddlesome toward the artist. We continue so to this day. Coventry Cathedral is an example. One of the most imaginative things that the Church of England has done for a very long time is to take the bold step of not only creating a new cathedral out of the ashes of the old but of finishing it totally in the short space of half a decade. The result is, of course, that the new Coventry Cathedral is in some ways an uncomfortable place to enter. After all, it hasn't been prayed in; it hasn't yet become an instrument of worship. Nevertheless, it is still a profoundly moving place. And it is instructive and rather chastening to walk around Coventry Cathedral and send your antennae up and listen to what is being said by sightseers. On a recent visit, I followed one couple. The woman was quite obviously a pillar of the Mother's Union, and her rather submissive husband was listening to what was essentially a one-way conversation. At last, as they paused

beneath Graham Sutherland's superb tapestry behind the
altar (one of the great moments of insight there), the worm
reared up and turned. "All right," he said, "I know it's
magnificent, but I don't like it."

Actually, he was speaking for many hundreds who go
around Coventry Cathedral. He may actually have been
both more instructed spiritually and more holy than his
wife. It wasn't for me to judge. But I am quite certain that
there spoke pious Philistinism, and it is precisely that attitude and that tone which is so profoundly dangerous for
the artist.

Patronage is a very delicate matter as it is exercised between persons. Some of the results of it were to be seen in
Wichita, Kansas, where the Liturgical Conference was held
in November, 1962. In the conference exhibition of art
and architecture, one could see, for instance, the subtly
delicate way in which an individual artist such as Wichita's
own Tom Krosno had been able to distinguish between
one commission and another. One could examine the precise suitability of three chalices he had beaten out—for a
university chaplaincy, a larger church, and a mission
church.

There is a kind of fidelity to the exact need of the particular individual Church in each work which the artist of
integrity creates. Compare this with the blundering uni-
formity with which our typical ecclesiastical furnishers attempt to make every church look like every other church.

But one should go a step further than that, and point to
the very core of the relationship—or, better, the "dialogue"
—between the artist and the living Church. We cannot
have clear living theology formulated in astringent, abstract

concepts. And our theology will not make its full impact on either clergy or laity, so long as we submit ourselves to debased icons and debased words.

At some time or another, all of us have probably marveled at the way in which a theologian or a liturgiologist may be able to make the finest, most hairsplitting distinctions. He may be able to define a doctrine with absolute precision in terms of the twentieth century. He may be able to tell you within one-tenth of a biretta's breadth the depth of a genuflection. And yet in spite of all that, he may totally fail to see that he is surrounded by icons—visual symbols —that are an insult to God and man, in their bad taste or total ugliness.

And we have not yet come to realize that this is an affront to the faith that we profess. Now this is not entirely a matter of ugliness, or of taste; indeed there is a lot of ghastly good taste in so many of our Churches. This is so frequently a matter of perceiving our Church in the past tense rather than the present tense.

New York provides as good an example as either England or Wales. There is something profoundly strange in sailing up the Bay towards the Manhattan skyline, seeing there a glorious carved jewel in architecture, a massive tribute not only to the technology of the twentieth-century milieu in which we live but also to its artistic sensitivity. To see the Manhattan skyline in the morning's dawn is a very fine experience. Then you go into the Anglican Cathedral of St. John the Divine and realize that your leg has been pulled, for here is a Cathedral whose builders pretend that it was built 300 years before Manhattan was thought of. The men who designed this Cathedral were copying, not creating.

You can create only in terms of the era in which you yourself live and think and of which you are a part.

This is the kind of thing, of course, that goes on throughout our Churches. We have all seen Churches built during our own lifetime with pretensions that their perpendicular architecture dates back to just before the reign of Henry VIII. We can see Anglican Churches, Roman Catholic Churches, Methodist and Presbyterian Churches pretending that they live in an antiquity which is, to say the least, utterly un-American.

In precisely the same way a new parish or mission in England will attempt to look neo-Gothic in a wildly inappropriate way. One would like to see some of the people who perpetrate these anachronisms made to walk around in chain mail or to celebrate the Holy Mysteries with Elizabethan doublet and hose beneath their cassocks. It is no exaggeration to say that this is precisely the intellectual attitude to which they are submitting themselves. They are copying, not creating.

Now, this may be amusing when we contemplate it at a distance. It is tragic when we think of what it is doing to young sensibilities. It is tragic when we think of what it is doing to that taste which is part of our belief and is a tacit assumption about the nature of God and of all that is visible. If it ever occurred to us of what wonderful masculine beauty God incarnate was when he moved among men; if we only realized what it meant to look on the face of Christ and see there unfallen man: we would perhaps be much less prepared to submit to fallen art—something that has only the thorns of creation. If only we could think a little more of these things and a little less of a bogus antiquity!

Now, can we assume then that there is dialogue between

ourselves and the artist? Can we assume that the artist has something to say to us as we have something sacramentally to say to him? If we are prepared to speak, the one to the other, something very considerable can happen.

THE FIRST LEVEL OF DIALOGUE

This dialogue can proceed at four main levels. *First,* there can be the dialogue between the Church and the artist who is totally committed to the sacraments and creeds of the Church and where, therefore, there is perfect accord between the artist and the living Church. Then, when the commission comes, when the Church exercises patronage, each party of the patronage knows precisely what is happening. The artist works inside the terms of the Church and the Church accepts the terms of the artist, for both are speaking a common language. Now, that can happen today. Consider four lines from the most distinguished of our poets in English, T. S. Eliot—an American who returned to his cultural, spiritual, and mental base. When he returned to East Coker and saw from what he had come, he was able to make the pilgrimage from there to Little Gidding. And when he arrived at Little Gidding, this was his insight:

> You are not here to verify,
> Instruct yourself, or inform curiosity
> Or carry report. You are here to kneel
> Where prayer has been valid.

Couldn't one read that as a little epigraph to a conference such as the one in Wichita? Ponder these brief lines for a moment: "You're not here to verify, instruct yourself, or inform curiosity, or carry report. You are here to kneel where prayer has been valid." This is a Christian talking

to Christians. He knows the common terms. He has been
to Little Gidding in the east of England where prayer has
been valid, and he has been prepared to kneel.

In Chapter I, Dr. Shepherd draws serious attention to
the ways in which we can be so concerned with externals
that we fear and fail to see the internal movement of the
Spirit. In the realm of liturgy, this can happen all too
readily. The forms and movements, ceremonials, and even
rites, can become hardened into matters of mere form. This
is dangerous.

Now let us imagine for a moment that in the ninth
century in the little cathedral city of Orleans, we are at-
tending an Easter morning liturgy. In the ninth century, the
liturgy had already taken a set form. And yet, on that Easter
day in Orleans, there happened something that had not
happened before in the liturgy. Out of the choir stalls there
proceeded three priests. They had drawn their amices up
over their heads, and they proceeded up to the altar where
there were three other priests waiting for them. And there
suddenly appeared, out of the Introit of the Easter liturgy,
a play. Here, *in toto,* is the whole of the first religious
drama that was ever written:

> *"Whom seek ye at the Sepulchre, O followers of Christ?"*
>
> *"Jesus of Nazareth who was crucified, O celestial ones."*
>
> *"He is not here. He is risen. See where He was laid."*

That was the beginning of all drama in the Church, and
we know pretty precisely when it began. What happened
was this: a liturgy that had perhaps begun to look a little
crystalline began at that moment, just at that single point,
to dissolve and move out—to send out little artistic tentacles.
And in that development of the Introit into what we call a

trope, the Church was beginning to see how part of its Easter liturgy could be dramatized.

For the next five centuries those tropes grew and developed until we had, by the end of the Middle Ages, a developed Christian drama. At that point the Church said, in effect, "Thank you, artist. Thus far, no further. The play has now become greater than the liturgy. Out you go, please, into the secular world. That is now your place."

Now, that is not only unseemly but indecent. That is not a proper dialogue between the artist and the living Church. The artist comes into the liturgy and says, "Please give me elbow room. *Move* inside the rite. Begin to *move* inside the ceremonial. Be dramatic about it, and then you will see how the liturgy comes to life." Would to heaven some of our bishops would see when they talk about liturgies that perhaps inside the rite a little dramatic movement could take place which might even border on the dangerous. But if it actually did become dangerous and got out of hand, as it did in the fourteenth century, then the proper place for it would be the market place. Meanwhile the liturgy would have heard a living word.

We can now bear, perhaps, to come back to the twentieth century. My own particular specialization is the theatre. I'm very proud that I have perhaps more friends among dramatists—actors, actresses, scene designers, and the rest—than I have among academics and priests. These are the people who speak my other language. My earnest hope is that out of those two languages, a dialogue can develop and be sustained.

If a greater number of our liturgical specialists who today speak of participation in the liturgy, and who like their altar to be central, should just occasionally attend a theatre-

in-the-round—in Stratford, Ontario, or Stratford, Connecticut, or the Circular Theatre in Ohio—in order to see what
the secular man is making of participation in communication, it is virtually certain that our liturgical considerations
would be greatly illumined. They would be able to see,
in clinical abstraction, what the theatre is seeing, both of
advantage and disadvantage, in this circular motion about
a stage. And they might see, also, some of the snags that
beset the Celebrant at the altar, even though he may very
properly be more concerned with his prayers than with his
dramatic movement. This again is an opportunity for dialogue between the committed artist and the committed
Church.

Finally, while we are still considering this first level of
dialogue, let us look briefly at a poem in the ancient and
lovely language of Wales. In medieval Wales, a courtly poet
called Tudur Aled was on one occasion writing a complimentary ode to the Bishop of St. Asaf. In the course of the
ode he likened the bishop to St. Augustine, to Alexander
the Great, and to a number of other secular and sacred
heroes. And then he addressed him directly. Translated into
English, this is what he said:

> Two circles placed on white,
> Beneath the sacrifice of
> The gracious and Holy God.

Now those lines puzzled medieval Welsh scholars for
quite a long time. Finally I had the enormous excitement
of being asked whether I could explain their meaning. To
a priest they are, of course, perfectly straightforward. "Two
circles placed on white, beneath the sacrifice of God, gracious and Holy." These are obviously the two little marks
left on the fair linen cloth as the priest's hands press down

upon the sacred vessels at the Consecration. This poet clearly knew his altar. He had been about the Holy Things, and when he addressed a complimentary ode to his bishop those were the terms in which he instinctively spoke. The dialogue was easy and gracious. It took place, to use Eliot's words, where prayer had been valid.

THE SECOND LEVEL OF DIALOGUE

But there is a *second* level of dialogue. The artist may not always wish to speak directly to the Church. He may regard it as his mission to speak to the Church *obliquely.* Look, for instance, at the careers of two of our most notable religious dramatists in England. T. S. Eliot begins with *The Rock* and *Murder in the Cathedral.* Then he moves out into *Family Reunion, The Confidential Clerk,* and all the other plays. That is to say, he moves from Canterbury Cathedral to Shaftesbury Avenue and Broadway. And this perhaps salutary move for the artist may even be a salutary move for the Church. This is mission activity.

Or let's take the career of Christopher Fry. He began with *The Boy with the Cart,* a work for the nave. He moved out into *A Phoenix Too Frequent,* a gay interpretation which the critics never saw, a kind of resurrection parable if ever there was one. He progressed to *The Lady's Not for Burning, The First Born, The Dark Is Light Enough,* and then *Curtmantle.* Progressively, it was a moving out into the world.

Each of these two notable dramatists has remained a Christian poet. Their work, their *dialogue,* has latterly been not with the institutional Church but with that part of the Church which is exercised with the world outside. At this point, two questions can be raised. We have already

examined those words from *Little Gidding,* "here where
prayer has been valid." But let us listen next to that terrible dialogue in *The Family Reunion*—probably T. S.
Eliot's dramatic masterpiece—between Agatha and Harry.
Harry is not at all sure whether he is guilty or not guilty
of the sins of his family. And Agatha, after a long and
terrible conversation with him, is persuading him that he
had perhaps better regard himself as—and this is the phrase
that she uses—"a bird flying through the purgatorial
flame."

When Broadway and Shaftesbury Avenue heard that
phrase, "it's a bird flying through the purgatorial flame,"
the audience, if it were sufficiently acute, could have seen
all of these relationships reflected in it: the Phoenix rising
from the flame as a symbol of resurrection (which is the
way the early Church saw it); of purgatory and its burning
flame; of individual purgation; of the waste land and of
the waste sea; of the way in which Coleridge's "Ancient
Mariner" has to go out into constant purgation; and of
Eliot's own progress through the waste land to Ash Wednes-
day. And if the audience were sufficiently acute to see all
that, then the Church, through Eliot, would really have
been having a valid dialogue with the world. It is vastly
preferable that Eliot wrote *The Family Reunion* for the
secular theatre than that we should produce any number
of pious little playlets in our parish rooms, to which the
world never comes—perhaps fortunately for us, or it might
laugh its head off.

Or, to go one step further, in *The Dark Is Light Enough,*
Christopher Fry makes what is apparently an absolutely
unambiguous statement of a secular dilemma that great
numbers of us have known. It was certainly a dilemma of

the thirties in Europe. He imagines two people married across frontiers, the Hungarian married to an Austrian. The unsatisfactory little Hungarian, Getner, comes back fleeing from the Austrian armies. And there is one awful moment in the play—it's one of the very high moments that Christopher Fry has achieved in the theatre—when Getner stands in the middle of a half circle of people gazing in contempt at him. He's gradually losing his nerve and at last bursts out to them in a moment of absolute hysteria, "Go to your imaginations, gentlemen. Think of death by shooting." And one of them withdraws and says, "I had rather weep for stags or partridges." And at that moment, when the contempt of one man has answered the fear of another, the Countess in the play responds by saying "Do then. Weep for what you can. It's grateful to our brevity to weep for what is briefer."

Was there ever a better expression of Christian compassion? Has the living theatre, the secular theatre, ever heard charity more succinctly expressed? If you can't weep for a man, if you haven't pity for a man in distress, and if you're one of the hearty type who can weep far better for a stag or a partridge on the wing, do then, weep for what you can. It's grateful to the brevity of human life to weep for a life that is briefer. At that moment, Christopher Fry reached a very high point in the dialogue between the artist and the Church. There was no need for him to come into a nave or a chancel in order to speak those words. He was speaking right there in the living theatre for the whole Christian tradition of compassion and charity.

And then, finally, let us consider the greatest play that he has yet written, *Curtmantle,* where repeating the course which Tennyson, T. S. Eliot, and Allcott followed in look-

ing at the argument between Thomas Becket and Henry
II, Fry dug much deeper than his predecessors into this
conflict between flesh and spirit, between law and charity.
He expressed for our day that conflict which the Church
always knows between equity, right, and compassion.

That is the *second* level of the dialogue between the
Church and the artist—a level at which the Church speaks
to a committed Christian, who answers not to the Church
directly, but rather to the world.

THE THIRD LEVEL OF DIALOGUE

Let us now consider the *third* level of dialogue. It occurs
during those moments of latent Christian insight that remain to the artist who has temporarily—or perhaps even
permanently—suspended his Christian belief. One can imagine the body of James Joyce stirring very restlessly in his
grave if anyone were to suggest that he had been a pious
Christian. But if one reads Joyce carefully, his work
throughout reveals reverberations of the Christian faith
which his native Ireland had implanted in him, willy-nilly.

Looking at what the other fellow is thinking is frequently
profoundly instructive for us and part, indeed, of our necessary missionary activity. It has always been a matter of
astonishment in the senior common rooms in which I've
worked that I have consistently urged that the senior common room not limit its newspaper subscriptions to the
Times and the *Guardian*. Not that they aren't all right.
But one already knows what the *Times* and the *Guardian*
will say. In addition to these, the one paper I wanted to
see every day was the *Daily Worker*. I knew what my *friends*
were thinking; but I wanted particularly to know what the
other fellow was thinking.

The Church too rarely is concerned with the thoughts of others. We are terribly self-satisfied and smug. We are quite prepared to enclose ourselves in the safety of our sanctuary and to be assured that nothing at all is happening outside.

But if you read James Joyce, Samuel Beckett, Shelagh Delaney, or Bernard Kops—people who have repudiated their religion or perhaps never even had it—you are then in contact with living artists whose integrity may be every bit as high as yours. They have their fidelity to their truth as they see it, and if you don't see that fidelity you will not be able to speak your truth to them.

Now in the light of that, let us look at one or two of these people and see what their truth is. One of the greatest creative geniuses that America has produced during this generation is that willful creature, Ezra Pound. I got to know him very intimately during his period in St. Elizabeth's Hospital in Washington, D. C. I felt it as great a privilege to speak to him every Saturday and Sunday afternoon while I was living there as to meet a great number of more honored citizens of that great city. From him I heard Christian insights about the nature of *usura,* the besetting sin of our society, which were very remarkable. It would do us all much good to go back and read Cantos XL to L of his massive work, especially that great Canto XLV which begins with *"Usura"* and ends with the passage beginning with the biting phrase *"Contra naturam."* It is frequently only the artist who can see the cancer in the bone. This particular artist, perhaps very flawed and deliberately an outcast, nevertheless had some insights that it pays Christians to see.

Let us turn next to a poem by the very considerable Welsh poet, Dylan Thomas, "Do Not Go Gentle Into That Good

Night." Americans know the wild Dylan Thomas who came very much adrift indeed in the United States. But I knew the background of this man. I was born some ten miles from his birthplace; he was of my generation. I knew the kind of family, the pious, intense nonconformity, the close puritanism of Welsh descent in which he had been brought up. And I also knew something of the kind of rebellion that he himself stood for. But read that little poem of his, "This Bread I Break":

> This bread I break was once the oat,
> This wine upon a foreign tree
> Plunged in its fruit;
> Man in the day or wind at night
> Laid the crops low, broke the grapes joy.

> This flesh you break, this blood you let
> Make desolation in the vein,
> Were oat and grape
> Born of the sensual root and sap;
> My wine you drink, my bread you snap.

There's a man who had repudiated Christianity but, my word, Christianity was in the very bones of him. It was in the blood that flowed in his veins, and he was more than acquainted with the Eucharistic sacrifice.

But let us go back to "Do Not Go Gentle":

> Do not go gentle into that good night,
> Old age should burn and rave at close of day;
> Rage, rage against the dying of the light.

> Though wise men at their end know dark is right,
> Because their word has forked no lightning they
> Do not go gentle into that good night.

> Good men, the last wave by, crying how bright
> Their frail deeds might have danced in a green bay,
> Rage, rage against the dying of the light.

Wild men who caught and sang the sun in flight,
And learn, too late, they grieved it on its way,
Do not go gentle into that good night.

Grave men, near death, who see with blinding sight
Blind eyes could blaze like meteors and be gay,
Rage, rage against the dying of the light.

And you my father, there on the sad height,
Curse, bless, me now with your fierce tears, I pray.
Do not go gentle into that good night.
Rage, rage against the dying of the light.

Dylan Thomas' father is on the point of dying, and if one looks at just the first three stanzas and the last, one sees something of the triumph of this man as he both repudiates a Christian death and at the same time uneasily realizes what a good end is. He knows what it is to die in the odor of sanctity, even though he is smiting the face of that sanctity as he writes. Consider the two puns in the first line. "Gentle" as an adverb and "gentle" as a noun—my "gentle father" and "gently": Do not go, gentle one (as it were) into that good night and "Do not go gently into that good night." And then there is the second pun "into that good night"—"good night" being both a farewell, and a reference to the darkness of death.

Let us consider the poem even more closely, because now we are looking at the dialogue of the artist to the Church. This is the artist saying, even though he doesn't realize it, "Thank you for the images you gave me. Here they are, rendered back. A little different but with perhaps a little grace, too."

Dylan Thomas is looking at his very saintly father, the father whom he respected, the father who was brought up in the piety of Welsh nonconformity. We hear the echoes of Old Testament theology as well as New in that "curse, bless, me now." We can almost hear Isaac, Jacob, Abraham, and all the other prophets. We can hear them both curse and bless in the Old Testament. And the son who is waiting at the death bed of his father pleads angrily, "Curse, if you wish, bless me now, but don't go gently into that good night. You should rage because there's more to be done." Well, of course, there speaks the good humanist.

Don't we, who hope that we might be good Christians, also wish that there were more than twenty-four hours in every day and that we would never permit ourselves to go gently into any good night but rather would work ourselves to the bone—because that is sacramental living?

The rage that Dylan Thomas speaks of is the rage at death. But the Christian knows, or ought to know, the other side—sacramental relaxation. He knows what it is to be quiet and withdrawn. Unhappily Dylan Thomas did not have that grace. Perhaps, please God, he has it now.

THE FOURTH LEVEL OF DIALOGUE

There is a *fourth* and final level of dialogue. At this level there are people who are not like Joyce, Pound, and Dylan Thomas—people who have retained vestiges of the faith even though they repudiate its corpus. Instead, they give every evidence of being outside the faith. And yet we should read what they have to say. How many Anglicans would think it a naughty or even downright sinister suggestion that they read a play by Bertolt Brecht? After all, he was writing totally behind the Iron Curtain. The majority of Anglicans are quite likely to say that it would be far more seemly to read St. Theresa, St. John of the Cross, or perhaps St. Andrew. But there is important exploring to be done by the Church into the matter of desolation, dereliction, of what it is to be out in the waste. This is where a play like Brecht's *Der Gute Mensch von Sezuan* becomes enormously enlightening. Look at it, and one develops a little more compassion and understanding of what it is to be without the faith and to be searching for it. One understands a little of what it means to be a Christian or, perhaps even more, a non-Christian beyond the Iron Curtain.

I knew, for one short while, some of the Berlin ensemble who played all of Brecht's plays in East Berlin. I saw one of the first performances of Brecht's *Das Verhoer des Lukulus.* I happened to be wearing clericals in this marvelous little theater in East Berlin. Some of the Communists, I must say, looked rather askance at this curiously dressed individual there. They perhaps wondered what I was doing. But it was a very moving experience to explore dereliction beyond the reach of our faith.

Or take the United States. Have we really seriously considered what a Christian has to say to, and about, Tennessee Williams? And hear from him? One will not understand America's contemporary culture without knowing what he has to say. Furthermore if, with patience and care, you read *Camino Real* you would understand what a present-day repudiator of the faith makes of *inferno, purgatoria,* and *paradiso.* Read the three acts of that play and see whether it isn't perhaps a more seemly approach to Dante in our twentieth century than the traditional academic or "scholarly" one. And if you don't know what I mean, read the play anyway.

Or if one would like to see the darker matters of Puritanism from which much of our pragmatic faith came, read the anthologies of Perry Miller. They throw considerable light on the puritan consciousness of New England.

Even better—read Arthur Miller's *Crucible* and see how the mind of a twentieth-century man with no faith in God works his agonizing problem through to a conclusion which is, at least temporarily, satisfying. I have a great deal more respect for the agnostic writer, or the agnostic painter, who works out the implications of his own art with inflexible fidelity to the truth as he sees it, than I have for the wishy-washy, spineless art which we foist on a great number of our people. *Camino Real* and the *Crucible* deserve much more respect than most of our unpleasant little nativity and passion plays which do no less than parody the faith of the Church.

This is the kind of approach that the artist of integrity forces upon us. He makes us see how the icons and words of another time and place cannot be refurbished for our day without losing their integrity. We invite an architect to design the structure of our worship-machine. We may then, as an act of very gracious charity, invite an artist to decorate it. We may even ask an artist, if we are very affluent and are in a very good mood, to provide us with vestments and vessels. And then, after that, we are content with debased music and with words that are unvital.

Compare, for instance, the poetry of Ezra Pound—whom so many Anglicans would repudiate with pious horror—with some of the flaccid, unprepared words that are so frequently delivered from our pulpits. Compare some of the words of Tennessee Williams, when he is analyzing the ills of the society which he sees all about him, with the words even of some of the prayers which we use in our non-liturgical services. Do this, and an honest Christian conscience is bound to admit that the artist has the better of the dialogue.

And if that is so, then that is a matter for very serious

penitence on our part. It is a matter for looking at this dialogue again. Our task is not so much the mission of the Church to the artist as it is the free, spontaneous, respectful, perhaps grave, perhaps gay, dialogue between the Church and the artist, between the artist and the Church. If that dialogue is spontaneous, and if it is mutually respectful, then it can be one of the most creative experiences that the Church can know in the twentieth century. And we shall perhaps find ourselves talking living sense about our liturgy. We may, indeed, eventually have a liturgy to which we can confidently invite our artists and ask them if they will not participate with us to the greater glory of God.

CHAPTER IV

THE CHURCH'S MISSION TO A SCIENTIFIC CULTURE

by

William G. Pollard

Ever since the close of World War II, it has seemed natural to everyone to speak of our time as "the scientific age." It is indeed an age in which throughout the whole world, free and communist alike, science has come into full flower. The great atomic energy national laboratories such as the one at Oak Ridge, the enormous high energy particle accelerators such as those at Berkeley and Brookhaven, the space rocket installation at Cape Canaveral, and many other large and complex installations are outward and visible signs of the triumph of the spirit of science in our culture. Big science mushrooms everywhere. The inner dynamism and power of the age derives from scientific aspirations and achievements, and it is science more than anything else which constitutes the unity and the passion of contemporary culture.

THE SCIENTIFIC PENTECOST

All this has been accomplished through a spirit which has been at work with power in Western culture for three centuries. The founding of the Royal Society in London in 1660 was like a second Pentecost. The spirit of science was given to man then, and it has grown with vigor and at a steadily accelerating pace ever since. Now that it has come to full flower and carried the whole of our culture along with it, it is time for us to consider the meaning of science for the mission of the Church in a culture so dominated by it. We are all familiar with the similar power which Christianity possessed to completely transform Classical culture into Christian culture in the three centuries between Pentecost and the Emperor Constantine. What can we gain by way of insight into the peculiar problems of the mission of Christianity in our age from this analogy between Christianity and science? Each grew with great power within an alien culture and in just three centuries of gestation succeeded in capturing the hearts and aspirations of all the people to such an extent that they came to dominate the whole civilization within which they were planted. Is there a clue here to the discovery of the key for the mission of the Church in this age of science?

In order to pursue this line of inquiry, we must first try to identify the special task which each had to perform in the culture which provided it with its peculiar mission and transforming power. For science this has been the illumination of the structure of the world of nature and the uncovering of the existence of timeless universal laws which govern events in space and time. Earlier, for Christianity this was the illumination of the structure and character of the supernatural and transcendent world through the revelatory power of the recognition of God incarnate in Jesus Christ.

Stated in this way, these two missions are seen to be clearly complementary, not contradictory or mutually destructive as is so often supposed. It is possible to know a great deal about the reality of nature and yet remain blind to the reality or even the existence of super-nature. It is equally possible to know much about what is regular, repeatable, and lawful in phenomena, and yet remain blind to the meaning of the singular, decisive, and revelatory events which stand out and mark the great turning points in individual lives and in history as a whole.

One hears much these days about the "conflict" between science and religion, as though they dealt with alternative, or even contradictory, views of the same area of reality. But this is to misconceive completely the true nature of the crisis of our age. The tension in which each stands against the other is of a quite different origin. We must see this clearly before we can begin to consider fruitfully how this scientific age may recover the capacity which Western culture so recently possessed to respond fully to the richness and fullness of the Catholic faith.

BONDAGE TO THE SPACE-TIME CONTINUUM

Science for all its wonderful achievements has been steadily leading our culture into an ever increasing bondage to the space-time continuum within which that portion of reality which we call "nature" is confined. Each generation during the rise of science has had less capacity than the last to respond to and maintain an awareness of reality transcendent to nature. The three centuries of the rise of science have been at the same time a journey into the intellectual and spiritual prison of our present bondage to space, time, and matter. For all their scientific brilliance, they have been years of gathering darkness as the real and substantial existence of the supernatural has slowly faded and disappeared. Modern man has become a complete solipsist with respect to the whole range of mankind's traditional and age-old experience of the invisible and unseen world transcendent to nature. As the vast reaches of space, measured in billions of light-years, have been opened through science to man's apprehension, the domain of reality within which space is immersed and which everywhere interpenetrates it, as would other dimensions perpendicular to it, has correspondingly shrunk to nothing. There is no place left for heaven, and modern man cannot even conceive of any way of getting out of space or of any reality not contained within it. In like manner as the vast ranges of time, measured in billions of years, have been opened by science to man's apprehension, so much the more has the dimension of eternity perpendicular to time faded from our apprehension.

As far back into the roots of human experience as archaeology has been able to take us, man's apprehension of the unseen world of supernatural reality has been as lively and vivid as that of the seen world of nature. In art and literature, in music and poetry, in liturgy and worship, among all races and cultures from the most primitive to the most advanced we find the evidence of this central fact of human experience. Indeed the function of the arts and poetry has always been to provide the means by which men could share and communicate with each other their experience of the supernatural, in the same way that mathematics and conceptual language is the proper means for sharing and communicating our experience of nature. Yet art predates language as a medium of communication among early cultures and was developed naturally and independently among all of them of which any appreciable trace has been preserved. Throughout the whole wide range and diversity of human experience, with the sole exception of the West in the nineteenth and twentieth centuries, the natural world has been alive with, and immersed within, a supernatural world which everywhere made contact with it, although transcendent to it. It is this whole dimension of reality which the scientific age has lost the capacity to experience or know.

THE CONTEMPORARY DARK AGE

An age such as ours which has lost a genuine capacity otherwise possessed by even a portion of mankind for knowledge and response to some great segment of reality is, without knowing it, truly a dark age. There is, of course, so much sparkle and achievement in twentieth-century science that it seems incredible to speak of this century as a dark age. Yet I am convinced that several centuries from now in the retrospect of history it is bound to be recognized as such, in spite of all its admitted accomplishments in the area of the natural. We really have lost a genuine capacity which the rest of mankind has possessed and actively exercised. We are a people trapped and in bondage within the prison of space, time, and matter. The very achievements which make this the golden age of science have led to this imprisonment and made it at the same time a dark age.

Consider for example the contrast between the age of Shakespeare at the dawn of science and our present day.

Surely much has been gained in the interval by way of insight into the structure of nature and the laws by which nature is governed. Doubtless, at that time there were many superstitions, errors, and unnecessary fears which science has by now largely dispelled. But just as surely much more has been lost by way of access to all that lies beyond nature. We are today still ardent advocates of the arts—music, poetry, and painting—but they have now all become no more than outward expressions of an inner world of the artist's subjective emotional experience and lively imagination. The external reference in supernatural reality has vanished, and there is nothing left to express save an illusory world inside man himself. America today is said to be quite religious, and the post-war religious revival is frequently cited in support of this contention. But at the same time religion is quite generally regarded throughout our culture as a purely private and inner manifestation of man's subjective experience with no external reference in objective reality. Much is said these days about the importance of values. Since, however, there is nothing discoverable by science within the world of nature in which any value system could be rooted, the only seat for values which remains is man himself. Thus we live in a culture for which the arts, religion, and values would all vanish from the universe should man perish from it. This is the dark age: the bondage to the natural; the imprisonment within the limited domain of space, time, and matter of which we have been speaking.

THE CHURCH'S MINISTRY TO THE DARK AGE

Against this briefly portrayed background of the character of our contemporary dark age, let us consider some of the implications for the Church's ministry to such an age. Of primary importance is the difficulty which such an age experiences with the great supernatural events which constitute the heart of the gospel: the incarnation, resurrection, and ascension of our Lord. So long as the material universe in space and time was quite naturally thought of as immersed in a larger reality, the event in which the Son of God "came down from heaven, and was incarnate by the Holy Ghost of the Virgin Mary, and was made man" could acquire its central place in the scheme of things as a real event in the real history of this world. But in our age even the bare idea of heaven as a real mode of existence transcendent to the space-time continuum has been largely lost. Viewed from within the prison of the modern scientific age, no transcendent domain of reality exists at all out of which the divine Word could come into space and time and be made flesh. In such a restricted framework of reality, the incarnation is simply impossible as a real event. Even those who accept its truth propositionally often experience difficulty in giving it substantial meaning within the framework of reality as they conceive it.

We are all aware of the widespread difficulty which the resurrection presents to the modern mind. The key to an understanding of the real source of this difficulty is the recognition of the extent to which the scientific age is actually a dark age as we have described it. It is clear from all of the accounts in the New Testament of the post-resurrection appearances of our Lord that Christ was raised into a new state of being no longer subject to the limitations of his earlier incarnate existence in the flesh. The resurrection of our Lord is a very different event from the raising of Lazarus, who was only restored to this mortal existence for a brief additional period, and in time had to die again. The risen Christ, however, could appear and disappear at will—even in closed rooms—and thus had been raised out of death into a mode of existence no longer confined, as we are, to three-dimensional space and time. As so many of the Easter hymns proclaim, the resurrection was a bursting forth from the prison of space, time, and matter into a wider, freer, and eternal mode of existence which God has prepared for all who believe in his Christ and trust in his power to raise them out of death where Christ has led the way.

Much the same can be said of the ascension. To the contemporary mind which, as we have seen, has become largely incapable of conceiving any transcendent or supernatural mode of real existence, the ascension can be interpreted, if at all, only as an event within space and time. In such a framework it cannot, of course, be regarded as an actual event, and so must be demythologized, as Bultmann has in fact done, in order to make it acceptable to a scientific age. But actually the ascension is in fact our Lord's final translation out of space and time. Instead of a movement upwards in ordinary space, it was a translation outwards along a perpendicular, if you wish, to three-dimensional space and time. During the forty days of his risen life, our Lord moved freely into and out of our world. The ascension is not essentially different in character from any of these other instances. It was simply that then the disciples knew that he would not return again in the body, but would thereafter be free to be present supernaturally in the breaking of bread everywhere and always, whenever and wherever the Holy Eucharist was celebrated.

A striking commentary on what the scientific age has

done to imprison the mind and spirit of man is provided by the contrasting responses of two Russian leaders to the results of missions carried out under their direction. In the tenth century Vladimir of Kiev sent emissaries to Constantinople, where they experienced the supernatural power of the divine liturgy in the Haggia Sophia. They returned to report to him: "We thought we were in heaven; for it is impossible to find so much magnificence on earth. We believe that we were there in the presence of God and that the worship of other countries is totally eclipsed." Vladimir had himself and the people of Russia baptized, and the Russian Church was established. In the twentieth century another leader, Khrushchev, sent Titov and other emissaries on a mission high above the earth into orbits around it. They returned to report to him that there is really no heaven and no angels, only more of the same kind of space and matter as we have here. Khrushchev is urgently engaged in trying to disassociate his people from the Russian Church. In the intervening centuries, the world of nature has been vastly opened up to man's apprehension, but in the process he has almost completely lost his former easy access to the world of super-nature.

OPENING MAN'S EYES TO TRANSCENDENT REALITY

In all previous ages for which the visible natural world was alive with transcendent supernatural dimensions, the response to the gospel was conditioned only by conviction with respect to the validity of the apostolic witness. It is a very different matter, however, to spread the gospel in an age which has lost the capacity to respond to any reality beyond space and time. To me this forms the central concern around which the mission of the Church to this scientific age is to be defined. Before the great revelatory events of the central drama of the faith can be meaningfully received again, it is first necessary to open men's eyes so as to behold once more the reality of things invisible and unseen. This in turn means, as we shall see, that the mission to this age must be primarily liturgical, rather than theological, homiletic, or pastoral as is often thought.

Before taking up the role of liturgy, however, I should like to speak of the effect of the loss of transcendent reality on the meaning of sacraments. Quite clearly it is only in a framework of reality in which the world of nature is everywhere in immediate contact with supernatural reality that the idea of the sacramental can be given any content. If there is no real mode of existence beyond space, time, and matter, then the bread and wine of the Eucharist, which are certainly material objects in space and time, cannot in themselves become anything else. Their sacramental quality, together with the real presence of Christ in the Eucharist, must then become purely subjective experiences within the individual worshipers without any real or objective status. This is indeed the only meaning which many people today can conceive for the sacramental, just as it is equally for art, poetry, and music. Only as the sense of the reality of transcendent dimensions, of numinous overtones throughout nature, is recaptured, can the full scope and meaning of the sacramental be truly appreciated. In a sacrament the natural and the supernatural meet and coalesce to produce a single reality which bridges the visible and the invisible worlds. In the present dark age, however, for which supernatural, invisible reality has largely vanished from our apprehension, all that is left in a sacrament is the outward and visible sign.

In this connection, I am reminded of a remark made by the philosopher F. S. C. Northrop some years ago. In a lecture devoted to the contrast between Eastern and Western thought, he commented on the extraordinary difficulties encountered in introducing Western technology into India. Even a simple thing like oiling agricultural machinery is extremely difficult to get Indian farmers to do regularly. In the oriental framework of reality, the material universe in space and time is ephemeral and illusory, a wholly subjective product of the human imagination. This, of course, is the precise opposite of the modern Western mind for which the transcendent, supernatural world has this same status. Hence, although you can teach Indian farmers exactly how to oil a piece of machinery, you can never be sure they will continue to do it after you have gone. The reason is that the oriental mind sees no possible connection between the application of oil and the functioning of the machinery. The act makes no sense to them and seems in their scheme of things a purely symbolic act.

In order to drive this point home, Professor Northrop remarked that the application of oil to machinery is for the Eastern mind no more intelligible than the application of water to a baby in the sacrament of baptism is for the modern Western scientific mind. This comparison brings out in an illuminating way the bondage of Western man to the category of the natural which constitutes our contemporary dark age. To a mind so imprisoned, Holy Baptism does not make any sense and can only seem a purely symbolic act, a pretty ceremony, having no effect on the child receiving it. In the same way, to the Oriental mind for which only the world of the spirit has reality, the process of oiling seems purely ceremonial without any effect on the machinery to which the oil is applied. When later the machinery breaks down, it never occurs to the Oriental to look for rust and corrosion as the cause. Rather he would be convinced that the real cause was spiritual, and doubtless demonic. In the same way for the Western scientific mind, when later on the person breaks down, the cause would never be thought of in terms of sin and judgment. Rather we are convinced in our scheme of things that the true cause must be sought in terms of neurological mechanisms and expressed in the categories of science and psychiatry. This contrast brings out in a particularly striking way the incapacity of those who are born into the modern scientific culture to fit the sacramental into their limited and restricted framework of reality.

It should by now be clear from all this that the key to the mission of the Church in the scientific culture lies in the recovery of our lost access to transcendent reality. Much contemporary apologetics fails, it seems to me, to see the importance of this. Without such a recovery, the existential truths of the Bible, the meaning and status of persons, worship, morality, and values, have no portion of external reality within which they can be rooted and grounded. They are all forced into the status of the subjective, inner, and private, while the real world around us continues to be the exclusive domain of nature which it is the special province of science, not revelation, to elucidate. The passion for science and the dominance of scientific standards of judgment flourishes in our culture with an inner dynamism and vigor which seems impervious to all arguments against it.

Even people within the Church are profoundly affected by the scientific age in which we all live. Although they enjoy life in the Church and are responsive to some aspects of Christian teaching, much of the fullness and richness of the Catholic faith remains inaccessible to them. The reason for this state of affairs ultimately goes back to the absence in our culture of any feel for the transcendental, supernatural, and eternal domains of reality.

LITURGY THE PRIMARY MEANS OF MISSION

Now if we ask by what means this mission can be carried out, it seems clear that the task falls primarily on the Church's liturgical ministry. It is chiefly in the celebration of the Holy Eucharist that art, music, language, and action all combine to make manifest the mystery of supernatural and transcendent reality as a direct, vivid, and living experience. No amount of preaching, of study, or of direct pastoral confrontation can make up for the absence of such direct experience. Only in worship, and here primarily in corporate liturgical worship, is the divine presence known in its actuality, the reality of spirit grasped, and the union of nature with supernature realized. What has been lost from contemporary culture is an elementary human capacity which all mankind up to a century or so ago quite naturally and effortlessly possessed. This elementary capacity, which Rudolf Otto has so aptly described as the numinous experience of the *mysterium tremendum,* is not easily recovered within a culture which has lost it. It cannot be taught or brought back by argument, and there is no program which the Church can formulate and put into action for its recovery. It can only be awakened by grace through the mutual contagion of the Spirit, and then only slowly

and in a few scattered individuals as God permits. This is
why the task must of necessity fall to the liturgical ministry
of the Church. Only there are the essential elements for
such a reawakening to be found.

A warning about timing and the immediate effectiveness
of this ministry is essential here. We have made the point
that the twentieth-century scientific culture, for all its bril-
liant achievements in understanding and controlling nature,
is nevertheless a dark age. Just as the first dark age arose
from the loss of the capacity to respond to the whole classical
humanistic Graeco-Roman heritage of Western civilization,
so the twentieth-century dark age arises from the loss of the
capacity to respond to the whole Biblical transcendental
Judaeo-Christian heritage of the same civilization. Now the
way out of a dark age is neither simple nor rapid. What
is required is a renaissance, a rediscovery of that which has
been lost. But a true renaissance is too profound a movement of the Spirit to be manipulated, programmed, or
pushed. The new renaissance which is now required, and
to which the liturgy of the Church has so much to contribute, is of this character. It must start slowly and spo-
radically, and its growth will be governed more by its own
inner strength and dynamism than by the calculated efforts
of those involved in it to push it. How long will be required
for it to reach full flower cannot be predicted at this stage.
At a minimum, however, it would seem to be several generations, and this means that none of us will see the fruition
in our lifetime.

To many in the Church this will seem a gloomy and
overly pessimistic conclusion. The insistent demand in the
Church today is for a plan of action which promises rapid
progress and quick results. To me, however, the situation

seems neither gloomy nor unreasonable. There is a heady
challenge with its own rewards in the vocation to be a
renaissance man in the midst of a dark age. I have not in
any way forsaken science or become disloyal to my earlier
vocation to it, as might be erroneously supposed from what
I have written so far in this chapter. I continue to rejoice
in its triumphs and to be thrilled by its achievements in
elucidating and controlling nature. But without losing any
of the certainly valid insights of science, what has happened
to me in recent years is that I have regained the equally
thrilling insight of the Christian revelation into the structure of supernatural reality by which so much of the life
of Western man has been lived but which I, with the majority of my contemporaries, had so completely lost. I find in
practice that the infection of this vision is difficult to trans-
mit to others, but occasionally it does happen. I rejoice
when it does, but I am otherwise content patiently to await
the development of the renaissance in which by the grace
of God I have been privileged to partake.

There are increasing signs in our day of a growing desire
to discover some means of escape from the dark imprisonment of the mind and spirit of man within space, time, and
matter which the rise of science has brought with it. The
scientific culture has again produced an age in which men
sit in darkness and in the shadow of death. It is certain that
man will not forever remain in this darkness. The renaissance of rediscovery of the wider range of external reality
beyond the domain of nature is already under way. Doubtless, like any renaissance process, its growth will be slow.
But that growth is certain and the full flowering of rediscovery within Western culture is assured. The mission of
the Church to the contemporary scientific culture is pre-

cisely to participate in and partake of this renaissance. Let
us not chafe and become frustrated with its necessary slow-
ness. Let us rather rejoice and be glad that God has chosen
to make us active participants in this great movement of
the Spirit within the twentieth-century dark age in which
he destined us to lead our lives.

CHAPTER V

THE LITURGY AND WORK

by

James A. Pike

"And then came Amalek and fought with Israel in Rephidim and Moses said unto Joshua choose us out men, and go out, and fight with Amalek: tomorrow I will stand at the top of the hill with the rod of God in mine hand. So Joshua did as Moses had said to him and fought with Amalek; and Moses, Aaron and Hur went up to the top of the hill and it came to pass when Moses held up his hand, that Israel prevailed; when he let down his hands Amalek prevailed but Moses' hands were heavy and they took a stone and put it under him and he sat thereon and Aaron and Hur stayed up his hands, the one on the one side, the other on the other side and his hands were steady until the going down of the sun and Joshua discomfited Amalek and his people with the edge of the sword."—Words from the 17th Chapter of the Book of Exodus.

A DICHOTOMY BETWEEN PRAYER AND WORK?

This passage from the Book of Exodus would, at first blush, seem to be a rather crude and superstitious story; it would seem to present a view of prayer which any sophisticated theology would reject. When Moses put his hands up, then right at that moment, more of the Amalekites got killed; and the minute he dropped his hands, the Israelites began to lose out. And then he puts them up, and things go well again; but when he drops them, things go badly again. This scene, in the "raw," as it were, presents a view of prayer which we generally preach *against* and yet which we must confess many of our people still hold; so one would want to reject the story out of hand. Also, those who have either pacifist tendencies or some sensitivity about warfare, whether because of a pacifist orientation or not, may be put off by the somewhat casual way the story ends, namely that "Joshua discomfited Amalek and his people with the edge of the sword." But if we look a little deeper, we will see in this narrative an image (whether an accurate historical account or not we don't know) of what liturgy and work mean in the biblical faith of the Holy Catholic Church.

The work at hand was to go into what is now Israel and a portion of the Kingdom of Jordan, develop this land, make it fruitful, and provide a home for a people under a special calling and under a special covenant. The fulfilling of this work was impeded by this difficult tribe—the Amalekites. The handling of this situation was, under the Providence of God, the immediate challenge. This was the work to be done—that the promises might be fulfilled, that the life in the promised land might be lived.

Most of those able to fight were out at the battle, but some were engaged in worship and in prayer. The relation between the two is somewhat obscured because of that specialization of function. That some work and some pray is (except in special circumstances) a false dichotomy. *Laborare est orare:* to work is to pray, to pray is to work. Yet, we will see the perspective more clearly because of the false dichotomy.

PROFESSION AND VOCATION

What is the work? What is our calling? Two words are used in English: *profession* and *vocation*.

We generally distinguish them in terms of the dignity or the clean-handedness of the job or the color of the collar. We speak of white-collar jobs and blue-collar jobs. Educationally speaking, we make a distinction between "professional schools" and "vocational schools"; it's nicer to be in a professional school than in a vocational school, the "smarter" people go to professional schools and not to vocational schools, etc.

Actually, however, from a Christian point of view, *vocation* is a nobler word than *profession*. Tracing it back to its root, a "profession" is what you hold yourself out to be. And hence, there are codes of professional ethics (for example, in my other profession, the law) which require the professional man to act in the way he has held himself up to be. The following of a set of rules will enable the practitioner to roughly approximate the established image. This is from the inside of you out. So once one decides to become a lawyer, get admitted to the bar, and hang out a shingle, one resolves to look like that thing that shows on the shingle —the thing which one has chosen to earn and obtain. But *vocation* is more than this. Its direct translation is "a calling." This, of course, implies a Caller. It points to something *outside of me.*

Actually the two words can be used of any work from

bricklaying to neurosurgery—*depending upon the way the worker sees his work.*

Without any supernatural level, without any doctrine of man, or of vocation, or of anything—simply as a minimum matter, we can expect people (decent people) to do what they say they will do: if they are going to lay bricks they will lay them decently. If they do not lay them decently, the contractor is let down, his expectations are let down, and in the end the worker may not even be able to continue in the work of bricklayer.

A good minimum level is a good place to start our action and our thinking. The doctrine of work under a world view including only the space-time continuum, as Dr. Pollard calls it in Chapter IV, would be roughly like this: good work is that which serves to enable one to keep going in the style to which one is accustomed—a "fast buck" or enough bucks to keep the show on the road, and/or that which is personally gratifying and pleasant to do. We could sum it up in the phrase "nice work if you can get it."

MADE IN THE IMAGE OF GOD

But the doctrine of work in the biblical faith is quite a different thing. This starts with the fact that we are made in the image of God. If we are so made, we should expect ourselves to function as we understand God to function. We don't know everything about how God functions: when we make these analogies, we must remember the limitations on our knowledge. As the author of the Book of Job puts it, "As touching the Almighty, we cannot find him out." Yet God has tipped his hand; he has revealed himself sufficiently that we can gain a clue as to what our imagehood means.

First, he is Creator. He not only created the world, he creates it. We read in Genesis that God was turning chaos into order. Well, that task is not completed; the world actually is quite a mess; and due to his gift to us of freedom, we are capable of turning what order there is back into chaos. Indeed we are now so scientifically skillful, particularly in the nuclear field, that we can pretty much turn the whole thing back into chaos.

But our calling, as made in his image, since he is Creator, is to be *creative*. We are meant to share with him in the task of putting things to rights—tidying up the universe. Hence, any field of work, from plumbing to atom-splitting, can be just that when seen in the perspective of sharing God's creative role in "ordering," for responsible purposes, the confusion, the mess in the world. So when an engineer uses his skills to dam a river which has been causing floods and destruction in order to make electric power for industry and to irrigate, he is sharing in the divine task of creation. And this is a holy thing, depending upon whether for him it is part of his calling or whether he sees himself doing merely what it says to do in the contract—in other words, practicing his *profession*.

Second, God is Redeemer. His redemptiveness was and is manifested primarily and uniquely in Our Lord Jesus Christ, through whom we see that God is, always was, and ever shall be. *We*, therefore, are called to be *redemptive*, we are called to be co-redeemers with him. We are called to heal, understand, pick up, lift up, hold on to, and fill the gaps between ourselves and others. The world is a very sick, sad, broken, hurt, wounded place; it is through *us* that God will heal and redeem. So, whether in the strictly pastoral role—as confessor or counsellor on the part of the priest, or in the work of the social case worker, the psychiatrist, the physician, or the friendly and loving neighbor, we are called to share God's redemptive work, by gearing our work to his whole eternal purpose, as co-redeemers with him.

Third, God is (and it is hard to find a fresh word for this) God is Holy *esprit de corps;* he is Holy Community Builder, Community Inspirer, "Joiner Together." Thus we are called to share in the ministry of uniting rather than dividing. We are called to bring people together, to be foci and centers of unity for those around us, joining with others on meaningful levels of common life and experience-sharing.

But also, we are called by the same Holy Spirit "who spake by the prophets" to transcend community and to judge community in terms of God's eternal purposes. "Be ye not conformed to this world," the apostle says, "but rather be transformed" and then go on to *transform it.*

We are called to share in the work of the Holy Spirit in building and judging community—to be part of and yet apart from the community, to be in the world, but not of it. While in the world seeking to help and to bring God's sons into meaningful and loving fellowship, we must be ready, nevertheless, at all times to range ourselves on God's side, against the community—sometimes even against the community of the visible Church.

VOCATION: THE CHRISTIAN MEANING

This then is our "calling." This is the Christian meaning of our daily work; it is a profound meaning which lifts us out of the realm of the "fast buck," or even out of the realm of "personal fulfillment," of which we hear so much these days. I do not ignore the values of a fast or a slow buck; I have four children and they all eat—this is fine. Personal fulfillment, yes: I have a job and I am glad that I have a job that I enjoy. And that is fine—there is nothing wrong with that. But when we look at it from the biblical perspective, that same work can have a much more profound meaning in terms of God's eternal purpose that the Creation be finished, that all men be redeemed and healed, and that all men be in community.

This which shall be the fulfillment is indeed the Kingdom come. It is a kingdom which can break through wherever we will let it: "The Kingdom of God is in your midst," our Lord says. Every time a broken relationship is healed, every time something is put to rights: *pro tanto*—for so much—the Kingdom has come, it has broken through right now.

Therefore, each of these acts of work under calling is part of the eternal purpose rather than merely part of the passing show.

Just take the matter of redemptiveness briefly. Suppose I am the agent through whom two persons who have hated each other come at least into an *agape* relationship of love —if not the stronger one of affection. Let us remember that agape is commended for us. If after we love enough in that way, we come really to *like* as well, that's an extra grace and blessing. There is no command to like anybody, but there is a command to *love*. If we achieve this in a particular case, this is *part* of what has to happen before God's will is fully done. If God is finally to be all in all, this is going to happen somewhere deep in heaven if it doesn't happen on earth. But if it happens on earth, *it has happened* and this fact is just as important as it would be should it happen in

heaven. All that happens now can be just as important as
it ever will be. We are *in* eternity, we are in this whole
stream of fulfillment of God's will, the completion of his
great, grand enterprise and scheme. And so when good
happens, it has happened, and it *is;* therefore, it is eternally
important. And the same is true of all the other things that
are part of our daily task—when performed in response to
God's calling us.

We have contrasted two different meanings of life and
work, depending on whether one is caught in the time-space
continuum—in a secular view of reality—or whether one
is caught up into the eternal view of reality and purpose
and calling.

"Moses held up his hands." There is no magic in this:
hands up, battle goes well, hands down, battle goes badly.
It would be very irreligious if that were the precise way it
worked. But let's take this ancient story at its best level.
When we live, figuratively speaking, with our hands up in
prayer and adoration—the seeing of the vision—then life
does have vast meaning. And when we don't live this way,
the meaning of life is puny, at best. When we live this
way, a task has glory, beauty, significance. When we don't
live this way, the same task is meaningless and turns to
dust.

ROOTED IN WORSHIP, FLOWERING IN ACTION

That's the point. In worship the first thing is *adoration;*
through it we see the real meaning, escape the time-space
continuum. No, we don't escape it; we stay in it. But we
also see more; we have "all this and Heaven too!" It is
through adoration that we can work out our calling in

terms of divine meaning. We adore God in both his Word and his Sacrament. For this reason, the Pro-Anaphora should not be regarded as the "preparation" for another thing that is *the* thing. Personally, I believe in the real presence of our Lord in his most blessed Word as I believe in his real presence in the blessed Sacrament: I bow as reverently when the Gospel Book is raised at the *Gloria tibi* as I bow at the Elevation at the end of the Canon of the Eucharist. Christ is truly and really present in the Word of God; and the Service of the Word is something that, having its own authenticity, can stand on its own feet. Through it we sense the presence of God, we see the vision, we see the larger picture, we praise him for his own worth, and we view a world which is his world and not ours alone. This is in one sense preparation for more, but in another sense, it summons us to our first calling. It is the first thing and, I suppose, in the end, the last thing in prayer and worship.

But it is true that in the full worship through both Word and Sacrament we go further. When we come to the Eucharist proper, there are three acts in the drama—Offertory and Penance, Consecration, Communion, and Thanksgiving. Let us consider these acts in an effort to tie the Eucharistic action to the doctrine of work.

When the alms and oblations are brought up, this represents, of course, the offering of the whole life—including the exercise of our calling. Making the total offering "in kind" would make the point more clearly but would be rather clumsy from a ceremonial point of view and clumsy in terms of the financial operation of the Church. I feel, especially now that I am an ecclesiastical administrator (a "prelate," as they say in the newspapers because that better

fits the headline space) somewhat like the officials of the
state of Nevada must feel as judged by the signs I hear they
put up on the roads: "Keep Nevada Green—Bring Paper."
But whether it be in kind or in paper, it does represent the
worshipers' life and work. St. Augustine in a sermon on the
Eucharist said in effect, in connection with what we call
the real presence: *you* are truly present on the altar.
Through these tokens you have offered yourself—the totality of yourself, not just your prayer life, not just your pious
moments, not just your hours or moments of reading the
Bible, or the liturgy or the Divine Office, but your whole
life, good and bad.

Now, the self in life and work is not an adequate offering;
hence, in the Prayer for the Whole State of Christ's Church
which follows as the continuation of the offering ("We
humbly beseech thee most mercifully to accept our alms
and oblations and to receive these our prayers, which we
offer unto thy divine Majesty") we take note of the weakness, the troubles, the divisions, and the sickness of the
world and of ourselves. So, we go right on and confess our
sins: the lives we offer are not even clean, let alone perfect
and complete. It is in this offertory action of the holy drama
of the Eucharist that we proclaim over and over again that
all we do—all our talents within our limitations, which
sometimes give a particularly sharp edge to our talents—
is frequently weak and inadequate and sinful, often wrong-
intentioned, and often based on mixed motives. But we also
proclaim that all of this is, nevertheless, under God's calling.

Now the second act. The continuing miracle of God's
grace—focused especially in the sacramental action, but
actually ever active—is that once we are dedicated to him

in this way, he accepts us and through our offering is with us in it all. We don't believe that through the Eucharistic action a spiritual presence floats around through the congregation. It is through these very tokens of bread and wine —which represent those very imperfect, indeed sinful, lives of ours, that God comes in actual fact and makes holy that which is inadequate, and yes, unclean.

Sanctity, holiness is this: the saint is not the *good* man; he is the *dedicated* man, the *"offered"* man. The more ancient the saint, the better he looks to us; we know less about him. Those we know a good deal about obviously were not totally and at all moments good. But they were dedicated; their lives were caught up in a commitment to God's purposes—and that is why "St." is put in front of their names. It is illuminating that in almost every language except English, "holy" and "saint" are the same word—"santa" in Spanish, for example. Thus, in the Diocese of California, which has such lovely place names, "Santa Clara" means *St.* Claire, and "Santa Cruz" means *Holy* Cross. Being a saint means being holy. The reason people say, "Well, I am not a saint you know!" is that they think that being a saint means being very good. But anybody can be a saint, because one can dedicate to God all he has and is, all his weakness and sins as well as his strengths. That is being holy—that is being a saint.

As we shall see in a moment, if *goodness* does not flow from this dedication one might question whether the dedication is genuine; "by their fruits ye shall know them," Jesus said. He did not say by your fruits you shall earn holiness; but rather by your fruits people will know whether holiness is there due to dedication. So this is the primary thing as far as our daily work's being holy, as far as our being saints, is concerned.

God does the rest; he accepts the unacceptable, enabling us to accept ourselves. Because of this precious gift we respond thankfully, inspired by a new dynamic for goodness, a new motive for eternally purposeful work. Our thankful response is expressed in the third act of the drama as we receive and express the desire to "do all such good works as thou hast prepared for us to walk in"—to do all to which he has called us. We want urgently not merely to live up to what we profess ourselves to be. We want to do the work to which he has called us, in the context of the vision we have seen in our adoration of him—the great vision of the God of history who cares about time and fulfillment now. We go on to offer ourselves—what we are as we are—to take our place in his divine scheme. Through his grace he sanctifies us; he makes holy whatever we are. Thus, in new confidence, with a new motive, and with renewed inner strength, we go and do the work.

Matching these three acts of the Eucharistic (and life) drama is Soren Kierkegaard's summary of the Christian religion: "The profound humiliation of man, the boundless love of God, and an endless striving born of gratitude."

Each of us is called to this whole pattern: *orare est laborare.* All of us, bishops, priests, and laymen alike, are called to work and are called to pray. Here our opening biblical image breaks down. All of us at all times, but especially in the Eucharist, hold up our hands and see the vision, and all of us, too, are called to be active in pushing aside the barriers to the fulfillment of God's great plan. When our hands are down, when we are not seeing the vision, our daily work is essentially meaningless, and indeed we may become cynical about it. When our hands are up our daily work is touched with glory, geared into eternal meaning and purpose; thus only are we fulfilled. Thus only can we fulfill our calling.

CHAPTER VI

THE CHURCH'S MISSION
TO OUR
URBAN SOCIETY

by

C. Kilmer Myers

The topic of this chapter—The Church's Mission to Our Urban Society—suggests that some definitions are in order at the outset. What is "The Church" which, presumably, has this mission? And what is "urban society?"

I am unable to answer these questions in full because I am neither a theologian nor a sociologist. They are difficult questions but none the less ones with which Christians in our day must be concerned continually. We must seek for answers old and new. We must look everywhere for people who possess answers, however partial. We must look beyond the rim of the Church's life for clues which have been hidden from us.

The answers to these questions will come to us not only through the writings of theologians and social scientists but also from the people as they live both in Church and society; in movements of people; in the caved-in in-

dividuals who walk alone on the city's streets; in gestures
both psychological and liturgical; in the way people talk
and herd together; in the posture of listening for hints of
goals and aspirations or the grim lack of them; and in the
pain of conflict and its separation of men. In short, the
answers come, fragmented to be sure, in the whole stuff of
life. Our chief difficulty may be that we often fail to understand them as answers even though they come screaming at
us by day and by night.

Often we are appalled at the complexities of our whole
technological society with its warring ideologies and ethnic
tensions. But as Christians we possess a sharply focused
light, which is Christ: a light showing us the way clearly,
keeping us from the precipice on either hand. This light
beams on, as we ourselves are grasped—as total men—by
the reality of Christ and his Body the Church.

And so definitions—in the sense of our being grasped by
reality—become the *sine qua non* of our action, our mission. First the tree and then the fruit. We become that
which we are. The beginning of answers, then, is found
first of all in Holy Baptism.

BAPTISM: THE PRIMARY SACRAMENT

The first and fundamental sacrament is Baptism. How
we have neglected this great sacrament in the primacy of
its place and meaning! Both in practice and in the pastoral
teaching of its role in the Christian life, we have relegated
it to the local sphere of the individual. The dominical command to "teach all nations" has come to mean baptizing
persons one by one. Baptism comes to mean the sacrament
of personal salvation. It is not related to the Mystical Body
because for us the Church is an *ecclesia ex animis,* i.e., the

Church of individual souls; whereas, of course, the Church is an *ecclesia ex gentibus,* i.e., the Church of peoples. Baptism is a social sacrament—the means of entrance into the Divine Society whose being is Christ. Baptism is the sacrament of transformation; its heart is the real presence which grafts the total man—himself the product of many—on to the true Vine. Baptism *nationalizes* us! It *colonializes* us! We become citizens of the Colony of Heaven set down in this foreign land which is our world, our urban society. St. John has the Lord of the Church say, "My Kingdom is not of *this* world." (John 18:36) St. Paul says, "The form of *this* world is passing away." (I Cor. 7:31, RSV)

Now, as I understand the New Testament, "this world" is not what we usually mean when in prayer and hymn we speak of a naughty, evil-ridden life of misery. Nor is "the next world" the place in which we begin to enjoy what the morticians these days call anew the "immortality of the soul." Rather, the focus of the early Christian writers is upon—in the words of John A. T. Robinson[1]—"the new resurrection order of 'life in Christ,' which they entered at Baptism and to which death could make no *difference*."

The resurrection order of "life in Christ" is entered through Baptism. All who pass through the waters of Baptism *are* regenerate, nationalized as citizens of the Kingdom of Christ. The celebration of the liturgy (in which we include Baptism as first and foremost in order) is the celebration of the holy gospel, the good news that salvation has been brought down from heaven to earth. The liturgy is the "social celebration of the mystery of Christian redemption, the royal way to the attainment of the true *salus*

[1] John A. T. Robinson, *On Being the Church in the World* (London: S.C.M. Press, 1960), p. 13.

publica, the public weal" [2] at the center of the social order, the urban society. In these observations, which need considerable elaboration, of course, do we find a beginning of answers? The forms of society change and will change. But the beginning in Baptism remains unchanged—one element in that sharply focused light which enables us to find the way in a difficult world. But this way we find *as a society* divine in origin and being, although living in the society of "this age."

Baptism is a key with which we may unlock our strategies —to use a word belonging to this age—as we move in mission toward the present forms of human society. Baptism is the revolutionary sacrament by which society is transformed. We must recover its revolutionary meaning and so restore this sacrament to its central position in the Church's life.

THE UNITY OF THE CHURCH

The crucial importance of Baptism appears when we consider the essential direction we must take as we move in mission toward modern (urban) society. This is the recovery of the unity of the Church. It is inconceivable that mission to urban society is possible for a fragmented Church.

During my ministry I have traveled back and forth across this country as an observer of and a consultant to groups concerned with the Church's mission to urban society. It may be said that almost without exception the chief obstacle to the formation and implementation of that mission is the disunity of the Church and the presence of churches. The voice of the Church is unheard by multitudes because

[2] *Orate Fratres,* May 16, 1937.

they hear only voices—the jarring sounds of separated com-
munities of Christians.

It is true that in America there are councils of churches.
But these councils—frustrated and inhibited by denominational self-interest and power interests—never speak with
the authority of the Church. In addition these councils are
ordinarily dominated by the ecclesiastical organization man
who never is really happy unless he is mimeographing in-
nocuous directives and at the same time slowly choking
himself to death with the red tape of bureaucratic machinery.

The theologically concerned Christian, the Christian
painfully seeking out the answers to real questions, is too
often absent from church council circles. He is not wanted
or he himself considers council meetings a colossal waste
of time. In our own Church the clergy and the laity involved in council activities are Episcopalians often farthest
removed from Anglican thought and practice. Many of us
are ardent ecumenists until we meet a Baptist in the flesh—
at some council meeting. But the fact remains that without
unity we are paralyzed in our efforts to meet the challenge
of the city. The Spirit moves, however, and today many
persons are searching for unity among Christians on the
deepest levels.

We must assert, first of all, that we men cannot "re-unite"
the Church. Neither can we rend it asunder. The Church
already is one because there is one Lord and one Baptism.

I would like to quote from a sermon I preached to my
former very urban congregation. The sermon was a comment upon the recent visit of the Archbishop of Canterbury
to New York City. The Archbishop had reminded us that
the Anglican Communion is a part of the one Holy, Cath-

olic and Apostolic Church of God. I said, "Sometimes this reminder comes as shocking news even to life-long Episcopalians. Many members of our Church think of themselves as 'Protestants' and that theirs is a 'Protestant' Church. We need to be reminded that nowhere nor at any time do we say, 'And I believe in the Protestant Church.' We confess, as we did this morning and do every day, that we believe in One Holy Catholic Church. One of our newspapers asked the Archbishop what he thought about returning to the Catholic Church. He replied with some emphasis that he never had left it.

"Every man, woman and child in this church this Sunday was baptized a member in the Catholic Church. *We all are Catholics.* If you were baptized with water in the Name of the Trinity in a Baptist or a Methodist Church or, as I was, in a Reformed Church, you were baptized into membership in the Catholic Church and you are a Catholic. All Christians (and only the baptized are Christians) are Catholics. In spite of many differences (some of them fundamental, to be sure) there is only *one* Church and that is the Catholic Church. There is only one Church because there is only one Christ. Do you remember the apostle's question, 'Is Christ divided?' (I Cor. 1:13)."

I went on to say that the only way to begin building the visible unity of the churches, the denominations, is for all to accept this fact: there is only one Catholic Church, and all baptized men, women, and children are members of it.

To this truth our Anglican Communion has been a constant witness, as our Archbishop reminded us. This truth rests upon the one Lord, the one Baptism into the resurrection form of life "in Christ." Dean Ladd used to say, "Unity is through Liturgy." The waters of Baptism are the creation of God alone; they are not manufactured or manipulated as are the bread and wine of the Eucharist. Unlike the Eucharist, man brings nothing to Baptism. Baptism is God's act alone.

Likewise, unity is God's act alone, assisted only by our assent to be baptized. Baptism is the sacramental and mystical action by which we are united with the Church— itself indissolubly united with the one Christ.

Recognition of this gives to us a sense of certainty in the ontological unity of the Church. Without that sense of certainty we are partially paralyzed and cannot act. It would appear that ours, more than any other, is the age of the Church in which action springs from being, the unalterable fact of the "mystical union betwixt Christ and his Church." Holy Baptism is the sacrament of unity. It therefore is the beginning of the divine strategy.

MAN'S HUNGER FOR UNITY

There is a deep hunger for unity in man. This may be said even in the face of ideological conflict and rampant nationalism. Disunity breeds guilt and despair. It creates the climate for conflict and bloody attacks of man upon man. Our technological society has created ultimate weapons of disunity, and peoples all over the world shrink with horror at the prospect of their use. At the same time technology has caused the world to be reduced in size; and with the population explosion we now crowd together.

The God who is the Lord of history works through all these strains and stresses to unite us. The key to this unity lies within the knowledge of the Church, although the Lord of creation also works outside the Church. In the Church, as Dr. Casserley reminds us, "The powers of the Kingdom are let loose." The focus of man's search for unity lies, therefore, in the Church—not the purely bureaucratic church nor the purely juridical church, but in the Spirit-filled Church of the Mediator. Mission can be thought of as no less than this. The Church is commissioned to "teach all nations." *The hunger of men for unity is, in fact, a hunger for the Church, the People of God.*

The millions of people who live in the world's cities hunger for unity. Meditate upon the hunger of the people of East Berlin and West Berlin. Think of the disunity of the people in the city which was my home for so many years, New York: ghettos separating one group from the others, community destroyed as though by deliberate plan, closeness of man to man only on crowded subways or in cliff-like dwellings. Consider the lack of legitimate opportunity for thousands of youths in our great cities and the consequent growth of delinquency. All of these city characteristics are signs of disunity. Whenever and wherever the possibility of a climate conducive to reunion appears, city people respond eagerly.

THE CITY AND ITS MASSES

But city people have no ideological center. They only live in cities. They are suspicious of power blocs which seek to unite them because of their past experience of being used as discardable pawns. City people are cynical of planners. They are no longer drugged by the promises of politicians—that is, until a crisis stirs them for a time out of their inertia. They live by a code which declares that anything is legitimate so long as one is not caught in the act. City people are lost in the complexity of the metropolis. The sense of being lost is heightened by machines and automation. The gains in leisure time are rendered mean-ingless by TV shows that insult the intelligence and by the aimless driving around in chrome-covered automobiles.

But they hunger and thirst after unity—personal unity. They hunger and thirst for the living God although they cannot call his name. They desire the Church—the Mystical Body which unites them with the Ground of their being.

These city people do not know the names of the symbols of the Church. Even many who belong to the Church do not know these names or symbols because the churches have drawn heavy curtains before them. The tradition of the Church is to many only a dim and distant echo. But the substance of the Catholic faith is known to them because of their bitter experience of disunity and their often uncon-scious desire for unity, for reunion, for community—for Holy Communion—in their lives. We must admit that if it were not for the Roman Catholic Church, only a tiny fraction of our city people would have even the memory of the Mystical Body of Christ. Despite our Anglican disagree-ments with Rome in certain points of both its theology and its devotion, we must unhesitatingly say that the Roman Catholic Church has kept alive in the hearts of millions the dimension of the Sacraments, the numinous in worship and, not least of all, a sense of unity in the world that crosses barriers of race, class, and nation. We only can stand over-whelmed at the vision of what a truly profound union of the catholic and reformed branches of Christianity would mean as the Church moves in mission towards modern urban society.

The city is more than building and hard pavements, bridges and expressways. The city, as Dr. Gross of Rutgers reminds us, has a psyche, a soul; it has a *geist*, a spirit.

These exist when there is a center about which its life re-
volves. These proceed from that vital center and are in some
way created by it. When the center is diseased and there
is no psyche or spirit, people flee the city. No longer is the
city the place where civilization is created. The city becomes an ant heap and then it dies. It might be argued that
all over our nation cities are dying because they have no
vital center. The center is a force, a power, which draws
those who inhabit the city into some form of unity. From
the unity flows the life-force of the city and its spirit. Could
it be that the cities in our Western world are dying because
the Church, its own life characterized by profound disunity,
no longer stands at the center of the city?

Our city planners think of the city in terms of redevelop-
ment and slum clearance. The primary instrument em-
ployed to effect these is the bulldozer. Areas in the city
which displayed some kind of communal feeling are bull-
dozed out of existence and people are scattered throughout
other parts of the city. Those who remain no longer trust
the community in which they have lived, perhaps for many
years. The old landmarks, however decrepit, are gone; and
gone, too, is the feeling of psychological security. The people who remain, and the people who leave, both feel root-
less and insecure. Many of us who have lived in these areas
sense a situation of hopelessness among the people. Even
the slightest will to be one's self vanishes, and only hostility
between groups and classes remains. This is the situation
in many of our great cities.

Finally, the poor and the rich remain while those in the
economic and social middle-class have fled to the suburbs.
These last still work in the city, but they do not care for
it. Sometimes they hate it. They look upon the poor as

enemies or as outcasts. They do not reach out to the poor and, by the poor, I mean the "city poor," those who are the victims of the planners. These poor victims are given little plots of green grass around their "project" buildings, but they are fined by the Housing Authority when their children stray away and put foot on the grass. These poor are numbers in the files of the great authorities. They live in numbered buildings on numbered streets. Their homes rest on a numbered floor, and on each door is still another number. When they want to be human they go back at night to some part of the old neighborhood that has escaped the planners and have a few drinks in a bar. It may be that they scream at each other and get in a fight; then they feel human and no longer fugitives from the housing police. It's a nice life in the inner city! And who the hell cares about it any more?

But it still is true to say that the cause of the Kingdom will be fought in the city. This has been true ever since the day the first Christ-bearers entered the slums of the cities of the Roman Empire. They had come from a series of mighty events which had taken place in another city called Jerusalem. Jerusalem! The archetype of the Mother of us all—the Church of Our Lord Jesus Christ! Is it any wonder that people in so-called slum churches sing with feeling,

> Jerusalem, my happy home,
> When shall I come to thee?
> When shall my sorrows have an end?
> Thy joys when shall I see?

They sing of the Church for which their souls long:

> There David stands with harp in hand
> As master of the choir: . . . .

Our Lady sings Magnificat
With tune surpassing sweet;

And. . . . Magdalen hath left her moan,
And cheerfully doth sing
With blessed saints, whose harmony
In every street doth ring.

This holy Church evokes no name in the minds of these
masses. We must help them to give her their own name.
This holy Church is the center, the vital center, from which
there proceed both soul and spirit for the city. The ancient
children of Israel fled from the blood-red cities of Egypt.
They passed through the waters of the Red Sea in order to
come at length to their new Jerusalem. Now today the
children of men must pass through the waters of Baptism in
order that they may be received into the congregation of
Christ's flock. This is the sign that they are regenerate and
grafted into the body of Christ's Church. We pray then that
all so signed may become what they have now become
equipped to be.

DEFINITIONS CATHOLIC AND RELEVANT

At the beginning of this chapter we raised the question
of definitions. To be defined were the Church, its mission,
and the urban society. Many who have read this far may
well be thinking that only the old definitions have appeared
and these in a somewhat archaic form. There is a sense in
which these people would be right. The only language I
know is that of the Catholic Church. I cannot jump out of
my own theological skin, and if I tried, the spectacle might
well be unedifying. If you will pardon reference to my own
thought evolution with respect to the Church's mission to
urban society, may I say that I am in revolt against those

THE CHURCH'S MISSION TO OUR URBAN SOCIETY

who say that the Church's only posture at this point is to listen, to listen to what the people on the assembly lines in Detroit are thinking and feeling. I'm all for listening (which, I take it, is learning to keep one's mouth shut). But I see no purpose in emptying one's self, even if one could, of those powerful symbols which have not only moved one's own life but that of Christians everywhere for almost two thousand years. Many of those who listen to city man, industrial man, technological man, New Yorker man, are themselves vacuous. We have a situation of one vacuum listening to another vacuum. Nobody says anything to anybody. But this is supposed to be "existential." And these days the moment you label anything "existential" no one is supposed to touch it. In much modern theological dialogue the way to win the argument is to call your opponent anti-existentialist. Try it; it never fails!

To return to definitions. The last thing I wish to do is to set forth a Tory theology of the Church and society. Nor do I wish to return to the Middle Ages. What I am trying to suggest is that it may be important for us to use the old-new substance of the Catholic faith as we seek to develop definitions that will grasp us and move us in the totality of our being.

Liturgically I was brought up by the Benedictines of Maria Laach. They speak of the *Mysterientheologie,* of the power of the signs and the symbols; they are anti-Franciscan. But I also was brought up liturgically by Dean William Palmer Ladd, who first introduced the Liturgical Movement to Massey Shepherd, to me, and to a host of others, including Ted Wedel. There was no one more impatient with those who persisted in putting new wine in the same old wine skins. He was a pioneer in so many ways and on so many levels. Not only was he a liturgiologist of the first rank, but he also believed in demonstrating the relevance of the Church's message to "real life situations." In his early days he was associated with Father Huntington on the lower East Side at Holy Cross Church. When I was at St. Augustine's on Henry Street, I thought of Dean Ladd almost every time I offered the Eucharist, because on the altar sat the tabernacle from old Holy Cross Church.

Those were the days on the lower East Side when Bishop Potter would spend a month in the rectory of a slum church in order to give the parish clergy a vacation. They were the days of Samuel Gompers and the Knights of Labor. When much later I was a seminarian I met up with the last few of these giants of the Church at meetings of the Church League for Industrial Democracy.

I'd love for Dean Ladd, if he were still with us, to meet and speak with some of the people who claim that the main function of the modern priest who has his eye on the mission of the Church to urban society is to adopt "a listening posture." What will they hear from the men who work on the assembly lines? What will they hear from the men on the executive level? They will hear practically nothing because neither of these groups has anything to say. Here is the real tragedy in modern urban society. *No one has anything to say.* It's all said for them by the ad men and by TV. We have reached, I think, just this point. Now, if you add to that sorry business a group of clergy with only shallow roots in the substance of the Catholic faith you have a picture of the current concept of the Church's mission to urban society.

But again I do not wish to be misunderstood. I am not saying that the way to implement the Church's mission to

urban society is to revive and refine traditional Anglo-
Catholicism. Lord Fisher tells us that this is an embarrass-
ment even to the Roman Catholics! No, there are a host
of priests like myself who midway through their active
ministry have no real home in any school of churchman-
ship. We cannot be Anglo-Catholics, and we cannot be
Evangelicals. We are a "third party" and find it a bit difficult to get better parishes. We cannot describe ourselves
and will not permit anyone else to describe us. The most
we can say is that we are "liturgical and Catholic; social
gospel and pentecostalistic!" We also have taken strong
doses of Protestant "protest." We cannot reject the Catholic
substance (a phrase, by the way, invented by a leading
German-American Protestant theologian). At the same time
we recognize the terrible difficulty in communicating the
meaning of that substance to modern men. The main reason for this difficulty is that the modern American city
man is now quite incapable of reacting to anything. The
gentlest judgment we can make of him is that he "is the
product of a sick culture."

DOCTRINE OF THE CHURCH IN URBE

Dean Ladd kept pulling us back to the doctrine of the
Church. In talking so much about the crucial role of Holy
Baptism, I have been following his teaching. Holy Baptism
is the fundamental sacrament of the Church. Much of the
meaning of the Church is to be found in it. But the Church
which Baptism reveals is not the Church of Americans let
alone the Church of American Christians, which, incidentally, is not the Church found in the Bible and the holy
tradition. The American Church, rather, is the answer of
modern men to the Church of Saint Paul. This latter

Church is the one which destroyed the Jesus of history and his simple ethic of love. Just as Saint Paul turned the Jesus of the synoptic gospels into the Christ of faith, so the fellowship of the disciples became the Church. The Church is pitted against the Kingdom. Almost all of us grew up with this kind of thinking. We never have gotten rid of it, despite its massive destruction by modern scholarship. One might say that not many of the scholars themselves have gotten over it. To most of our contemporaries, the Church remains something we can pick up or throw down at will. Never in American religious history has the concept of the Great Church been central. Dean Ladd used to tell us that if we were Catholics we could be anything. But we have not found it possible to be Catholics because we have not known the meaning of the Church. And so we are everything else *before* we are Catholics.

But the Church is because Christ is. She shares his Being, which is that of Very God who for us men and for our salvation came down from heaven and through the operation of the Holy Spirit tabernacled among us. In this vertical line of wondrous movement he crossed the line of our existence so that we were able to touch him. This is his Being—walking our roads, healing, teaching, suffering, weeping, dying, suffering his Body to be broken, becoming glorified broken Body—this is his Being which we saw and heard and touched and handled. And the Church in the mystical convolution of loving, divine acts is his Body! She is his Bride—bone of his bone, nerve of his nerve, flesh of his flesh. Each time I stand before a man and a woman to solemnize their marriage I speak those words which tell these two that their union is like unto the mystical union betwixt Christ and his Church.

The Church has many beautiful names. Men have whispered them, sung them, shouted them—Bride of Christ, Body of Christ, Colony of Heaven, People of God, Mother of us all, Jerusalem. Elsewhere I have written of riding in the train up from Gaza into the Holy Land. Up from the valley we climbed until the sun arose and there, golden in hue, wondrous in view, was Jerusalem. It was at that moment, I think, that I came to know what the Church is— the True Vine, the Community of the Redeemed, the Nation of Kings and Priests, resting upon the rock of God's mighty acts in our history.

Of course the Church is fallible; God judges her and chastises her. She makes colossal mistakes. She has promoted terrible injustices and has lived in torpor for decades. But at the same time—to cite the all-familiar paradox—her roots are found in the heavenly Being of Christ. As in the psycho-sexual unity of man and woman, beginning in a mythical garden where there were no barriers between man and man, or man and beast, or man and God, or, indeed man and himself, so the Church, beautifully arrayed in robes made white by the blood of the reconciling Lamb, continues this paradisical symbolism. In her the powers of the Kingdom are let loose. She is the extension of the powers of the Christ who himself is the Kingdom because she is indissolubly united with him. Her beginnings are to be found in pre-existence as well as in the whole history of man because she is God's wish and in him will and act are simultaneous.

She is not a voluntary society which we may take up or throw down. She was not created by man nor did we invent her. She is given and we come to her. She is here in power in the parishes of this city; she is present in power in a white-washed country Bethel. She is movement, endless procession, constant celebration of the passion, death, resurrection and glorification of the Christ who is one with her. Her history, as Calvin declared, is that of a succession of resurrections. She is everywhere—latent or manifest, hidden, or open. Often she is where the Lord's name never is spoken. She crowds in on us from every side. From her we first heard the words of life; within her we were washed with the waters of Baptism; at her tables we are fed with God's bread and from his cup; we are at home in this House, this City. We are at home because she is Christ's and Christ is God's. The Church is the Holy City Jerusalem, the Mother of us all.

Our vocation is to live in Jerusalem set in the midst of what Jane Jacobs calls the life and death of great American cities. The Church is a city in the midst of cities. The suburbs like to think that they have captured the Church— to scramble up Gibson Winters. The Church in the city is made to think that somehow it is inferior and a poor cousin. Think of the organization men who are vestrymen in the suburban parishes! But Jerusalem is a city; let us not forget that. It is where men are held close together, where sin is more possible, more complicated, more elaborate, that grace appears. It is under these conditions—the conditions of Harlem and Bedford-Stuyvesant, on the one hand, and the Lincoln Center, the Metropolitan Museum, and Greenwich Village on the other—that beauty and art and culture in all their complicated and wondrous forms may appear to be the teachers of the status-conquered, admen's victims of the suburbs. Here in the city, the City of God appears in all her beauty and power.

She appears first of all in her being. This is the manner in which she appeared in the slums of the cities of the Roman Empire. This is the way she appears now in New York, Johannesburg, London, and Peiping. Her great issues always are decided in the cities. If she leaves for a time to dwell in the desert or in the place of retreat it is only to return to the city where the people are with even greater power. Recently the Archbishop of Central Africa declared that the issue of Christianity and its struggle for the soul of Africa will be decided in the cities of Africa. The people are in the cities. The students march in the cities. The parliaments meet in the cities. The demons and the angelic powers are most active in the cities. We cannot forget him of whom it was said, in the time of greatest decision, that he set his face to go to Jerusalem.

THE STRATEGY OF THE SACRAMENTS

And so Baptism is the beginning of strategies. Baptism is entrance into the inner city, Jerusalem. It may be that there are different stages in Baptism; at least I have found it so during many years as a minister in the city. There is the kind of Baptism that occurs when a woman comes to you and in the tale of her awful life of rejection says simply that she found love first in the church of which you are pastor. The one I remember died before the waters could be poured over her head, but she had entered the holy city Jerusalem like Lazarus, who also was a poor man. There is the street gang which in the complications of its bloody encounters on the streets of the city finds, in its own way, the heavenly city. There is the artist who, without words, paints to the glory of God. He has found the Baptism, the unity, sought by all men everywhere. One cannot be statistical about it. The Lord of history never counted up his converts day by day, and even those he made ran away when the darkness fell. They found their way back. It all takes time, and each step forward is precious and of the utmost urgency when you are there to see it taken.

Baptism leads to feasting because it is such a happy event. The feasting goes on in the Eucharists offered in the Jerusalem set in the midst of cities. And let us not despair. The Church is God's, not ours. I baptized a boy once. Afterwards he asked, "God did it, didn't he?" I said, "Yes, he did it." The boy said, "I know it; everything seems different." God does it. God does it because he is God. We fail because we are men. God does it in us because he forgives us without any strings attached to that stupendous act. And so the Church *is*. She is; and Baptism, the Sacrament of unity, is the door through which the fragmented man of the city may enter to receive the new resurrection order of life "in Christ."

THE STRATEGY OF THE CATHEDRAL

There can be no detailed blueprint for the form which the miniature city of God, the parish, will take in the life and death of great American cities. It should be said that the parish not only will, but *must,* continue to be the basic cell in the mission of the Church to urban society. To be sure the parish, as such, is under heavy attack from several quarters. It is called obsolete and irrelevant to the human situation in the urban concentration. It is considered a hang-over from the town and country church.

No one will deny that the form of many city parishes is now obsolete. Every great city contains some obsolescent church units which are doomed to die. Some do not need to suffer this fate, and their loss would be serious.

Certainly each city needs one or more cathedral-type churches. These stand as witnesses to the Church's unitive function in the urban community. They need to develop specialized ministries. They may serve as houses for great acts of worship and as forums in which the debates of our time may be carried on. They should become known as centers of rich liturgical and artistic endeavor. Clergy who are able to preach with power and relevance should lead these churches. The other parishes in the city should help to support great churches of this kind, and efforts should be made to endow them. Our own Church with its many Cathedrals is in a position to offer leadership here for many other churches. In this connection, perhaps our own Anglican Church should seriously re-explain the office and function of the episcopate in the development of mission to the urban society. Our aim should be to free the bishop of those responsibilities which prevent him from being the father of the See city and the prophet as well. How wonderful it would be to see restored in some way the relationship between the bishop, the essential minister for most of Christendom, and the Sacrament of Baptism.

But certainly there is great power in the symbol of the Church's unity in the Cathedral. We must not, I think, use this in our effort to economize or modernize the church's system in the city. It is a question, rather, of a far bolder use of the imagination and a fuller use of the experience old and new in the employment of the symbol of the Cathedral. I am impressed deeply with the way in which some of our more imaginative deans are putting their cathedrals to work as centers both of liturgical life and of prophecy. We had one such in New York, but his vocation led him elsewhere. (See what he says about "vocation" in Chapter V.)

SPECIALIZED MINISTRIES

Another form of strategy is the development of specialized ministries. I am not proposing that we train clergy, for example, to minister among trade unionists. I am proposing that we train clergy to train laymen to minister as Christians among trade unionists. The priest here acts as a "resource man" in helping the laity to relate the philosophy and action of the labor unions to the theology and practice of the Catholic Church. The priest does not put himself in the position of "organizer" or advisor to trade union councils (an early mistake of the Jesuits in some of their Schools of Labor). He is not a leader at all in this sense. He helps train the militant Christian actionist.

Another example would be the "political specialist"—a priest trained primarily in the Christian and non-Christian uses of power in our modern urban-industrial complex. Here again, this specialist-priest would not "go into politics." He would train the laity to give expression to their ministry in the area of political thought and action.

It might well be that such specialists could move out from the cathedral or the cathedral-type church of the city. In this way each priest would be related to the power-center of the diocese and have an altar as well. Suffice it to say that we need to put our imaginative intelligence to work on this largely uncovered area of the Church's mission. Here also is an area in which ecumenical cooperation may well be possible.

THE EPISCOPAL ROLE

In our ecclesiastical tradition, strategy must of necessity center around the bishop. This suggests continued training and indoctrination of bishops. Many of our bishops, like many priests and laity, decide to act as though we still were a predominantly rural nation. They have little or no idea of the nature of urban-industrial social and economic dynamics. This being true, one needs to question seriously whether they are capable, without training and orientation, of developing a strategic mission to our urban society. Although I rather suspect that the suggestion of a training school for bishops will go over like a lead balloon, I nevertheless propose it in all seriousness. The kind of training given clergy going to the mission field by some of the Roman Catholic Orders might well serve as a model.

One other area in which specialization is needed is in keeping open the lines of communication with intellectual movements among American college students. I think especially of political and civil rights groups which exist in confusing abundance in cities like New York. The Church is only beginning to learn what is going on here. With few exceptions, the clergy carry on no dialogue at all with these groups.

PAROCHIAL STRUCTURE

Happily, our urban-directed strategy rests solidly still upon the parochial structure—that miniature Body of Christ which is the parish. We recognize that the parish is not able to perform specialized tasks—although more could be done on these levels if the clergy would cut out ruth-

lessly (and no matter *what* the laity says) many irrelevant
tasks. But the parish still is the symbol of unity in a culture
which craves unity so desperately. The parish still can be a
place of hospitality and acceptance in the cold urban society. There can be no question but that those parishes in
which the Church is renewed by the liturgy have engen-
dered a climate favorable to hospitality and acceptance.
This is true especially of many parishes in the inner city.

THE JOY OF MAKING EUCHARIST

One asks why this last is true. It is in part because in
these parishes there is a sense of crisis between the Church
and the world. There exists a tension between Jerusalem
and Babylon. The crisis may be racial or gross economic
and social injustice may precipitate it. Its presence in the
life of the parish causes liturgy to come alive. The crisis
causes the liturgy in some sense to become again the "secret"
thing Christians do—something is done "inside" the church
which is forbidden outside in the world. The parish in
which there is no sense of crisis between the Church and
the world is a dead parish. Each Mass sounds the note of
crisis. The crisis inherent in the world's life is each day
brought to the altar at the offering of the alms and oblations. Into the bread and wine, by the very act of their
manufacture, went the joy of nature, the love of man and
woman, the treasure of children, and the bitter rejections
of this world. When the offering is placed upon the Holy
Table, lacking the laughter and tears of man's life, the
Lord Christ again, it would seem, trudges to Calvary *alone*.

But because we are baptized into this death and resur-
rected life, because we forever are "in Christ"; he never is
quite alone. For, something of us is offered up in the sacri-

fice of the Eucharist and we *know* we are in crisis, that we share this final break with the world.

It was indeed a break. It was an act of love done in order that the world might be one—one with the Sacrificed even as he is one with the Father.

Baptism and Eucharist are eschatological Sacraments. They point to the end, to the new age of the new song when (as in Origen's vision) God shall be all in all and (in that of St. Augustine) there shall be one Christ loving himself.